Anonymous

Bible Songs - Consisting of Selections from the Psalms Set to Music

Suitable for Sabbath Schools, Prayer Meetings, etc.

Anonymous

Bible Songs - Consisting of Selections from the Psalms Set to Music
Suitable for Sabbath Schools, Prayer Meetings, etc.

ISBN/EAN: 9783744782784

Printed in Europe, USA, Canada, Australia, Japan

Cover: Foto ©Thomas Meinert / pixelio.de

More available books at **www.hansebooks.com**

BIBLE SONGS:

CONSISTING OF

SELECTIONS FROM THE PSALMS,

SET TO MUSIC.

SUITABLE FOR

Sabbath Schools, Prayer Meetings, etc.

*"Praise His name, young men and maidens,
Aged men, and children small."*—Ps. CXLVIII.

PITTSBURGH:
UNITED PRESBYTERIAN BOARD OF PUBLICATION.
Nos. 53 and 55 NINTH STREET.
1887.

FERGUSON BROS. & CO.,
ELECTROTYPERS AND PRINTERS,
PHILADELPHIA.

PREFACE.

THE General Assembly of the United Presbyterian Church, realizing the want of music adapted to the use of Sabbath Schools, at the meeting held in Cambridge, Ohio, in 1878, appointed a committee "to prepare and publish a book of selections from the Psalms set to music."

The committee thus appointed proceeded to do the work assigned, and reported to the Assembly that met in New Wilmington, Pa., in 1879. This Assembly directed the committee to publish their book "without any unnecessary delay."

This book is now offered to the public.

This work has not been done without continued labor, and earnest prayer for divine direction.

In making these selections from the Book of Psalms, it is not to be inferred that some parts of these Psalms were regarded as being more excellent than others, but only that they seem to be better adapted for use in Sabbath Schools. Many other selections might have been made with equal propriety, but this would have made the book larger than is necessary.

Music has been selected from almost every available source, and special care has been taken in its adaptation, so that the music shall express the sentiment of the Psalm to which it is set.

(3)

The best pieces of the old music, with which the church has long been familiar, have been retained. A fair proportion of new music has also been selected from the wide range of recent publications.

Thanks are due to D. C. Cook, Judge C. C. Converse, W. T. Wiley, J. W. Bischoff, and others who have generously granted us permission to use pieces of which they are the authors and owners. These pieces cannot be used by others without like permission.

It is not claimed that this work is perfect, but for the present it is the best that we are able to offer; and thus we cast our bread upon the waters, hoping to find it after many days.

COMMITTEE.

BIBLE SONGS.

No. 1. THE HAPPY MAN.

Ps. 1st, 1-4. C. M.

Rev. D. A. Duff.

1. How blest and hap-py is the man, Who walketh not a-stray In coun-sel of un-
2. Nor sit-teth in the scorn-er's chair, But plac-es his de-light Up-on God's law and
3. He shall be like a tree that grows Set by a riv-er's side, Which in its sea-son
4. And all he does shall pros-per well: The wicked are not so, But like the chaff be-

CHORUS.

god-ly men, Nor stands in sin-ners' way.
med-i-tates On his law day and night,
yields its fruit, And green its leaves a-bide,
fore the wind, Are driv-en to and fro.

The wick-ed are not so, The

wick-ed are not so, But like the chaff be-fore the wind, Are driv-en to and fro.

No. 2. HENDON.

Ps. 2d, 5, 6, 8, 9. 7s.

Rev. Dr. Malan.

1. Thus hath said the Lord Most High, I will pub-lish the de-cree: Thee I own my
2. Ask, for her-i-tage I'll make All the heathen na-tions thine; Thou shalt in pos-
3. Therefore, kings, be wise, give ear; Hearken, judg-es of the earth; Learn to serve the
4. Fear his wrath, and kiss the Son, Lest ye per-ish from the way, When his wrath is

Son, for I Have this day be-got-ten thee, Have this day be-got-ten thee.
ses-sion take Earth to its re-mot-est line, Earth to its re-mot-est line.
Lord with fear, Min-gle trembling with your mirth, Min-gle trembling with your mirth.
but be-gun, Blest are all that on him stay, Blest are all that on him stay.

No. 3. HEAR, O LORD.

J. L. BISCHOFF.

Ps. 5th, 1, 2, 3, 5, 6. 7s.

1 O Je - ho - vah, hear my words, And my med - i - ta - tion weigh;
2 In the morn - ing, Lord, my voice Thou shalt hear in sup - pliant cries;
3 Thou, Je - ho - vah, art a God Who in sin can - not de - light;
4 But in thy a - bun - dant grace To thy house will I draw near;

Hear my cry, my King, my God, For to thee, O Lord, I'll pray.
In the morn ing, Lord, to thee I will lift my wait - ing eyes.
E - vil shall not dwell with thee, Nor shall fools stand in thy sight.
To thy ho - ly tem - ple, Lord, I will look and bow in fear.

CHORUS.

Lead me in thy right-eous - ness; Ev - er - more my steps main-tain;

And be-cause of watch-ful foes, Make thy way be - fore me plain.

No. 4. LABAN.

DR. L. MASON.

Ps. 3d, 2, 3, 5. S. M.

1 My shield and glo - ry, Lord, Thou lift - est up my head.
2 I lay and slept, I woke, Kept by Je - ho - vah's care;
3 Sal - va - tion to the Lord A - lone doth ap - per - tain;

I cried and from his ho - ly hill The Lord me an - swer made.
Though myr - iads com - pass me a - round, Their hosts I will not fear.
Up - on thy peo - ple ev - er - more Thy bless - ing shall re - main.

No. 5. SAFELY GUARDED.

Ps. 5th, 9-10. 7s.

Rev. D. A. Duff.

1 But let all in thee who trust, Ev - er glad and joy - ful be;
2 For Je - ho - vah to the just Will a - bun - dant blessings yield,

Let them joy who love thy name Safe - ly guard - ed, Lord, by thee.
And with fa - vor com - pass him Safe - ly round as with a shield.

CHORUS.

Safe - ly guard - ed, Safe - ly guard - ed, Safe - ly guard-ed, Lord, by thee.

Safe - ly guard - ed, Safe - ly guard - ed, Safe - ly guard - ed, Lord, by thee.

No. 6. ENWOOD.

Ps. 4th, 5-7. L. M.

1 In sac - ri - fice of right-eous-ness Your hom-age to the Lord ex -press;
2 O who will show us a - ny good? Ex - claims the rest - less mul - ti - tude;
3 More joy from thee has filled my heart Than all their corn and wine im - part.

And ev - er let your heart re - ly With con - fi - dence on God Most High.
But lift on us, O God of grace, The cheer-ing bright-ness of thy face.
I lay me down to peace- ful sleep, For thou wilt me in safe - ty keep.

No. 7. DELIVER ME.

C. E. Pollock.

Ps. 6th, 1, 2, 4, 5. 8s &7s.

1 Lord, in an - ger do not chas - ten; Thy fierce wrath from me re-strain;
2 Sore - ly vexed by my op-press - ors, Grief like age has dimmed my eye.

I am weak; in mer - cy has - ten, O re - lieve my flesh from pain.
Hence and leave me, all trans-gress - ors, For the Lord hath heard my cry.

Sor - rows deep my soul are griev - ing; Lord, how long!— O pi - ty take;
God hath heard my sup - pli - ca - tion; My pe - ti - tion will not spurn.

Lord, re - turn, my soul re - liev - ing; Save me for thy mer - cy's sake.
Let my foes with sore vex - a - tion, Back in sud - den shame re - turn.

No. 8. ROCKINGHAM.

Dr. L. Mason.

Ps. 9th, 5-8. L. M.

1 The Lord for - ev - er shall en - dure, He hath for judg - ment set his throne,
2 Je - ho - vah shall a ref - uge prove, A ref - uge strong for poor op-pressed,
3 And they, O Lord, that know thy name, Their con - fi - dence in thee will place;
4 Sing prais - es to the Lord most high, To him that doth in Zi - on dwell;

In right-eous-ness to judge the world, And jus - tice give to ev' - ry one.
A safe re - treat, where wea - ry souls In troub-lous times may find a rest.
For thou, Je - ho - vah, nev - er hast For - sak - en them that seek thy face.
De - clare his migh - ty deeds a - broad, His deeds a - mong all peo - ple tell.

No. 9. LORD, OUR LORD.

Ps. 8th, 1-5. 7s.

By per. W. T. Wiley.

1 Lord, our Lord, o'er earth's vast frame, How ex-alt-ed is thy name!
2 From the mouth of chil-dren young, From the in-fant's lisp-ing tongue,
3 When thy heav-ens I sur-vey, Which thy fin-gers' work dis-play,
4 What is man that in thy mind He a con-stant place should find?
5 Thou his sta-tion didst or-dain Just be-low the an-gel train;

Who hast set thy glo-ry bright Far a-bove the heavens height.
Matchless strength thou hast or-dained, Thus, thy venge-ful foes re-strained.
When the moon and stars I see, Or-dered all by thy de-cree:
What the son of man that he Should be vis-it-ed by thee?
Glo-ry thou hast o'er him shed, And with hon-or crown'd his head.

CHORUS.

Lord, our Lord, o'er earth's vast frame, How ex-alt-ed is thy name!

Who hast set thy glo-ry bright Far a-bove the heavens height.

No. 10. BRIGHTON.

Ps. 10th, 16-18. S. M.

1 Je-ho-vah ev-er reigns, And firm his throne shall stand. The
2 Of those that hum-ble are, Thou, Lord, hast heard the prayer; Thou
3 To judge the fa-ther-less, And those by men dis-tressed, That

hea-then na-tions are de-stroyed For ev-er from his land.
al-so wilt pre-pare their heart, And still in-cline thine ear;
they by man that is of earth May be no more op-pressed.

10

No. 11. BREMEN.

Ps. 12th, 3-4. C. P. M.

Manhattan Coll.

1 "For those that are oppressed indeed, For all the poor that sigh in need,
2 God's words are pure as silver tried, In furnace sev'n times purified.

Lo, now will I arise;" Thus saith Jehovah in his grace,
Thou from this race, O God, Shalt keep thy servants ever more.

"And them I will in safety place From such as them despise."
When vilest men are raised to power, The wicked walk abroad.

No. 12. HINTON.

Ps. 7th, 4-6. 11s.

German.

1 Awake, that my cause may by thee be sustained, Awake to the
2 All nations of men shall be judged by the Lord; To me, O Je-
3 Establish the just, and let evil depart, For God who is

judgment which thou hast ordained, And then shall the people around thee draw nigh;
hovah, just judgment afford, According as righteous in life I have been,
just tries the reins and the heart. In God for defence I have placed all my trust;

For sake of them, therefore, return thou on high.
And ever integrity cherished within.
He saveth the upright, and judgeth the just.

No. 13. HOW LONG.

Ps. 13th, 1-6. 7s &6s.

C. E. POLLOCK.

1 How long wilt thou for - get me? Shall it for - ev - er be?
2 How long my soul take coun - sel? Thus sad in heart each day,
3 O Lord, my God, con - sid - er, And hear my earn - est cries;
4 Lest foes be heard ex - claim - ing A - gainst him we pre - vailed;
5 { But on thy ten - der mer - cy I ev - er have re - lied;
{ And I with voice of sing - ing, Will praise the Lord a - lone,

O Lord, how long ne - glect me, And hide thy face from me?
How long shall foes ex - ult - ing, Sub - ject me to their sway?
Lest I in death should slum - ber, En - light - en thou my eyes;
And they that vex my spir - it, Re - joice when I have failed.
With joy in thy sal - va - tion My heart shall still con - fide. }
Be - cause to me his fa - vor He hath so large - ly shown. }

CHORUS.

How long, How long, shall it for - ev - er be?
*I will praise, I will praise, will praise the Lord a - lone,

How long, How long,
I will praise, I will praise,

O Lord, how long ne - glect me? And hide thy face from me.
Be - cause to me his fa - vor, He hath so large - ly shown.

No. 14. MY HIGH TOWER.

Ps. 18th, 1, 2, 4. L. M.

W. A. TARBUTTON.

1 Thee will I love, O Lord, my might, My rock, my help, my sav - ing power,
2 I to Je - ho - vah lift my prayer, To whose great name all praise we owe;
3 Dis-tressed, I called up - on the Lord, And to my God ad-dressed my prayer;

My God, my trust, my shield in fight, My great sal - va - tion, my high tower.
So shall I by his watch-ful care Be safe - ly guard - ed from my foe.
My voice he from his tem - ple heard, My cry as - cend - ed to his ear.

* Chorus for last verse.

No. 15. WHO SHALL DWELL?

Ps. 15th, 1-5. 7s.

Rev. D. A. Duff.

Bass Solo. *Sing solo first and between each verse.*

O Je-ho - vah, who shall dwell In the tem - ple of thy grace?

Piano Accom.

Who shall on thy ho - ly hill Have a fixed a - bid-ing place?

1 He who walks in right-eous-ness, All his ac - tions just and clear;
2 He who ne'er with slandering tongue Ut - ters mal - ice and de - ceit;
3 Who the im - pi - ous will spurn, Hon - or those who fear the Lord;
4 Who no us - u - ry will claim, Nor with bribes pol - lute his hand;

He whose words the truth ex - press, Spo - ken from a heart sin - cere,
Who will ne'er his neigh-bor wrong, Nor a slander - ous tale re - peat.
Tho' he to his loss have sworn, Will not break his plight-ed word.
He who thus his life shall frame, Shall un-moved for - ev - er stand.

No. 16. TRUST HIS LOVE.

Ps. 16th, 7-10. S. M.

Rev. M. F. McKirahan.

1 The Lord be - fore me still I set, and trust his love; At
2 My soul in death's dark pit, Shall not be left by thee; Cor -

my right hand he guards from ill, And noth - ing shall me move.
rup - tion thou wilt not per - mit Thy Ho - ly One to see.

TRUST HIS LOVE.—Concluded.

Now glad - ness fills my soul, And joy shall be ex - pressed; My
Life's path thou wilt me show, To thy right hand me guide, Where

glo - ry shall his name ex - tol, My flesh in hope shall rest.
streams of plea - sure ev - er flow, And bound - less joys a - bide.

No. 17. LORD, HEAR ME.

Ps. 17th, 5-8. C. M.

J. M. Stillman.

1 Hold up my go - ings, Lord, me guide In paths that are di - vine,
2 Up - on thee I have called, O God, Be - cause thou wilt me hear;
3 Thy won - drous lov - ing kindness show, Thou, who by thy right hand
4 As th'ap - ple of the eye me keep: In thy wings' shade me hide

That so my footsteps may not slide Out of those ways of thine,
That thou mayst hearken to my speech, To me in - cline thy ear,
Dost save all those who trust in thee From such as them with - stand,
From wick - ed men and dead - ly foes Who rage on ev' - ry side,

That so my footsteps may not slide Out of those ways of thine,
That thou mayst hearken to my speech, To me in - cline thy ear,
Dost save all those who trust in thee From such as them with - stand,
From wick - ed men and dead - ly foes Who rage on ev' - ry side,

That so my footsteps may not slide Out of those ways of thine.
That thou mayst hearken to my speech, To me in - cline thy ear.
Dost save all those who trust in thee From such as them with - stand.
From wick - ed men and dead - ly foes Who rage on ev' - ry side.

No. 18. RESCUE.

Ps. 18th, 15-18. C. M.

Rev. D. A. Duff.

1 And from above the Lord sent down, And took me from be - low; From ma - ny wa - ters
2 They rose a-gainst me in the day Of my ca - lam - i - ty; But ev - en then the

drew me out, Which would me o - ver - flow. He me relieved from my strong foes, And
Lord him-self A stay was un - to me. He to a place where lib - er - ty And

such as did me hate; Because he saw that they for me Too strong were and too great.
room was hath me brought; Because he took de-light in me, He my de-liv'rance wrought.

No. 19. LISCHER.

Ps. 19th, 5-7. H. M.

1 God's per-fect law con - verts The soul in sin that lies; His tes - ti - mo - ny
2 The fear of God is clean, And ev - er doth en-dure; His judgments all are
3 God's judgments to the taste More sweet than hon - ey are, Than hon - ey from the

sure Doth make the sim - ple wise; His sta - tutes just de - light the heart; His
truth, And right-eous-ness most pure. To be de-sired are they far more Than
comb That drop-peth, sweet-er far. With coun-sel they thy ser - vant guard; In

ho - ly pre - cepts light im - part, His ho - ly pre - cepts light im - part.
fin - est gold in rich - est store, Than fin - est gold in rich - est store.
keep-ing them is great re-ward, In keep - ing them is great re - ward.

Ps. 17th, 1-3. C. H. M.

No. 20. CALM.

1 O Lord, do thou the right re - gard, And to my cry give ear;
2 When thou dost prove and try my heart And night - ly vis - it me,
3 As for the works of men, O Lord, Who seek my ov - er - throw,

From no dis - semb - ling lips, O Lord, Pro - ceeds my hum - ble prayer.
To search me in the in - most part, And all my thoughts to see,
I have pre - served me by thy word From paths where - in they go.

O let my judg-ment come to light, And let thine eyes be - hold the right.
Thou nought in me shalt find a - miss, For nev - er shall my mouth trans - gress.
Hold up my go - ings in thy way, And then my foot - steps shall not stray.

Ps. 21st, 1-4. 12s & 9s.

No. 21. ROWLEY.

1 Now the king in thy strength shall be joy - ful, O Lord, And shall in thy sal -
2 All the bless - ings he craved thou didst gra - cious - ly give, With the pur - est of
3 Through sal - va - tion from thee, has his fame spread a - broad, Thou didst glo - ry and
4 For the king, in the name of Je - ho - vah most high Did un - wav - er - ing

va - tion re - joice; For the wish of his heart thou didst free - ly af - ford, And re-
gold he is crowned; When he asked of thee life, thou hast made him to live While the
hon - or im - part; Thou hast made him most bles - sed for - ev - er, O God, And thy
con - fi - dence place; On the name of Je - ho - vah he still will re - ly, And shall

quest of his sup - pli - ant voice, And re - quest of his sup - pli - ant voice.
a - ges shall cir - cle a - round, While the a - ges shall cir - cle a - round.
pres - ence has glad - dened his heart, And thy pres - ence has glad - dened his heart.
stand ev - er - more in his grace, And shall stand ev - er - more in his grace.

No. 22. WHY STAND AFAR.

Ps. 22d, 1-6. L. M.

Prayerfully.

E. M. Clark.

1 My God, my God, why me for-sake? O why to me no ans-wer make?
2 Our fa-thers put their trust in thee, They trust-ed and thou didst them free;
3 "He trusts in God; let God de-fend And save him since he is his friend."

In deep dis-tress I cry, O Lord, Why stand a-far — nor help af-ford?
To thee they cried, de-liv'-rance came; They hoped, and were not put to shame.
Thou mad'st me first the light to see, In in-fant years to hope in thee.

All day, my God, I cry in vain, Nor can I in the night re-frain:
But I a worm, as no man prized, Reproached of men, by all des-pised;
From birth de-pend-ent on thy power, Thou art my God from childhood's hour;

But thou art ho-ly, who dost dwell A-mid the songs of Is-ra-el.
All shake the head, they mock and gaze, Each scorn ful lip con-tempt be-trays.
Be not far off: for trou-ble nears, And none to give me help ap-pears.

No. 23. OLIVE'S BROW.

Ps. 22d, 15-17, 19. L. M.

1 To thee in praise, I'll lift my song, A-mid the great as-sem-bled throng;
2 The meek shall eat till sat-is-fied, The food thy lib-eral hands pro-vide.
3 Earth's ut-most bounds shall hear and turn; All tribes and realms thy wor-ship learn;
4 A seed shall rise to serve the Lord, That race as his he will re-gard;

Where those that fear Je-ho-vah bow, I will per-form my sa-cred vow.
Who seek the Lord, shall him a-dore; Your heart shall live for ev-er-more
For God the Lord, all em-pire owns, And rules a-bove all earth-ly thrones.
They'll come and tell to sire and son, The right-eous deeds the Lord hath done.

No. 24. AGAWAM.

Ps. 23d, 1-3, 5. C. M.

Firm and strong.

W. B. B.

1 The Lord's my shep-herd, I'll not want. He makes me down to lie
2 My soul he doth re-store a-gain; And me to walk doth make
3 Yea, though I walk through death's dark vale, Yet will I fear no ill;
4 Good-ness and mer-cy all my life Shall sure-ly fol-low me;

In pas-tures green; he lead-eth me The qui-et wa-ters by.
With-in the paths of right-eous-ness, Even for his own name's sake.
For thou art with me, and thy rod And staff me com-fort still.
And in God's house for-ev-er-more My dwell-ing-place shall be.

No. 25 PORTUGUESE HYMN.

Ps. 24th, 4-6. 11s.

J. READING.

1 Ye gates, lift your heads, and an en-trance dis-play, Ye
2 What King of all glo-ry is this that ye sing? The
3 The King of all glo-ry high hon-ors a-wait, The

doors ev-er-last-ing, wide o-pen the way; The King of all
Lord, strong and migh-ty, the con-quer-ing King. Ye gates, lift your
King of all glo-ry shall en-ter in state. What King of all

glo-ry high hon-ors a-wait, The King of all glo-ry shall
heads, and an en-trance dis-play, Ye doors ev-er-last-ing, wide
glo-ry is this that ye sing? Je-ho-vah of hosts, he of

en-ter in state, The King of all glo-ry shall en-ter in state.
op-en the way, Ye doors ev-er-last-ing, wide op-en the way.
glo-ry is King, Je-ho-vah of hosts, he of glo-ry is King.

No. 26. EXPOSTULATION.

Ps. 24th, 1, 2, 3. 11s.

1 The earth and the ful - ness with which it is stored,
2 What man shall the hill of Je - ho - vah as - cend?
3 He shall from Je - ho - vah the bless - ing re - ceive,

The world and its dwel - lers be - long to the Lord;
For he on the seas its foun - da - tion hath laid,
And who in the place of his ho - li - ness stand?
The man of pure heart, and of hands with-out stain,
The God of sal - va - tion shall right - eous-ness give;
For this is the peo - ple, yea, this is the race,

And firm on the wa - ters its pil - lars hath stayed.
Who swears not to false - hood, nor loves what is vain.
The Is - ra - el true who are seek - ing thy face.

Ps. 25th, 1, 2, 5. C.M.

No. 27. REMEMBER ME.

C. E. Pollock.

1 To thee I lift my soul, O Lord: My God, I trust in thee:
  O let me ne - ver be a-shamed, Nor foes ex - ult o'er me.
2 O Lord, let none be put to shame Up - on thee who at - tend;
  But make all those to be a - shamed Who cause - less - ly of - fend.
3 Let not the er - rors of my youth, Nor sins re - mem - bered be;
  In mer - cy, for thy good - ness sake, O Lord, re - mem - ber me.

CHORUS.

Re - mem - ber me, Re - mem - ber me, O Lord, re - mem - ber me.

In mer - cy, for thy good - ness sake, O Lord, re - mem - ber me,

No. 28. MARKET SQUARE.

Ps. 25th, 3-6. S. M.

From the "Pioneer.

1 Show me thy ways, O Lord; Thy paths, O teach thou me; And do thou lead me
2 For thou art God that dost To me sal-va-tion send; And wait-ing for thee
3 Thy ten-der mer-cies, Lord, To mind do thou re-call, And lov-ing kind-ness-
4 My sins and faults of youth Do thou, O Lord, for-get; In ten-der mer-cy

in thy truth, There-in my teach-er be, There-in my teach-er be:
all the day, Up-on thee I at-tend, Up-on thee I at-tend.
es, for they Have been through a-ges all, Have been through a-ges all.
think of me, And for thy good-ness great, And for thy good-ness great.

No. 29. RANSOM ME.

Ps. 25th, 12, 13, 15, 16. 7s.

C. E. Pollock.

1 O my God, to me re-turn, Un-to me thy mer-cy show;
2 Let my soul be kept by thee; Res-cue me from all my foes;

I in deep af-flic-tion mourn, De-so-late and ve-ry low.
From con-fu-sion keep me free, I in thee my trust re-pose.

Griefs of heart are ve-ry great; Me from all dis-tress re-lieve;
Truth and right shall me de-fend. For on thee I ev-er wait:

Look on my af-flict-ed state, All my tres-pass-es for-give.
Ran-som, Lord, to Is-rael send, Him re-deem from ev'-ry strait.

No. 30. ADULLAM.

Ps. 26th, 2-5. C. M.

1 Ex - am - ine me, and do me prove; Try heart and reins, O God;
2 With per - sons vain I have not sat, Nor with dis - sem - blers gone;
3 My hands in in - no - cence, O Lord, I'll wash and pu - ri - fy;
4 That I, with voice of thank - ful - ness, May pub - lish and de - clare,

For thy love is be - fore my eyes, Thy truth's paths I have trod.
Th' as - sembly of ill men I hate; To sit with such I shun.
So to thy ho - ly al - tar go, And com - pass it will I.
And tell of all thy migh - ty works, Which great and won - drous are.

No. 31. GOD WILL NOT FORSAKE.

Ps. 27th, 9-12. C. M.

Mel. by J. B. Burley, arr. by M. V. Zimmerman, by per.

1 O Lord, give ear when with my voice I cry a - loud to thee;
2 When thou didst say, Seek ye my face, My heart did thus re - ply:
3 Far from me hide not thou thy face; Put not a - way from thee

Up - on me al - so mer - cy have, And do thou an - swer me.
Thy face, O Lord, a - bove all things, For - e - ver seek will I.
Thy ser - vant in thy wrath; thou hast A help - er been to me.

CHORUS.

O God, my Sa - viour, leave me not, And nev - er me for - sake:

Though pa - rents both should me de - sert, Je - ho - vah will me take.

No. 32. PRAYER AND PRAISE.

Ps. 28th, 1, 2, 3, 6. S. M.

1 O Lord, to thee I cry, Thou art my rock and trust; O be not si-lent,
2 O hear my ear-nest cry, Thy fa-vor I en-treat; Hear while I lift im-
3 O draw me not a-way With men who live in sin; Who to their neighbors

lest I die And slum-ber in the dust.
plor ing hands Be-fore thy mer-cy seat. } Now bless-ed be the Lord, Now
speak of peace While mal-ice lurks with-in.

bless-ed be the Lord, He heard me when I cried; Je-ho-vah is my

strength and shield, Je-ho-vah is my strength and shield, On him my heart re-lied.

No. 33. ZEBULON.

Ps. 27th, 3-5. H. M.

Dr. L. Mason.

1 { One thing I seek through grace, For this to God I pray; } To
  { That in his ho-ly place I ev-er-more may stay, }
2 { In times of trou-ble I In his pa-vil-ion hide; } A-
  { Safe in his tent I lie, And on a rock a-bide. }
3 { Lord, hear me when I pray, In mer-cy ans-wer me; } With
  { Soon as I heard thee say, "Seek ye my face," to thee }

see the beau-ty of the Lord, And in his tem-ple seek his word.
bove my foes he lifts my head, And I de-light his praise to spread.
pleas-ure did my heart re-ply, Thy face, Je-ho-vah, seek will I.

No. 34. BOW AND ADORE.

Ps. 29th, 1, 2, 5. 12s & 11s.　　　　Arr. by Rev. D. A. Duff.

1 Ye sons of the might - y, give ye to Je - ho - vah, O
2 The voice of Je - ho - vah comes o - ver the wa - ters; His
3 Up - on the great wa - ters Je - ho - vah is seat - ed. A

give to him hon - or and strength ev - er - more, O give to the name of Je -
voice o'er the vast and deep o - cean is heard: The God of all glo - ry is
King whose do - min - ion is nev - er to cease. Je - ho - vah with pow - er will

ho - vah due glo - ry: In beau - ty of ho - li - ness bow and a - dore.
speak - ing in thun - der; How might - y, how aw - ful the voice of the Lord!
strengthen his peo - ple; Je - ho - vah will bless all his peo - ple with peace.

Bow and a - dore, bow and a - dore, In beau - ty of ho - li - ness bow and a - dore.
The voice of the Lord, voice of the Lord, How might - y, how aw - ful the voice of the Lord.
Bless all with peace, bless all with peace, Je - ho - vah will bless all his peo - ple with peace.

Ps. 31st, 1-3, 5. S. M.　　## No. 35. FREEPORT.　　Arr. by R. B. Robertson.

1 De - fend me, Lord, from shame, For still I trust in thee;
2 Bow down to me thine ear, De - liv - er me with speed;
3 Thee for my rock I take, My fort - ress and my stay;
4 In con - fi - dence to thee, My spir - it I com - mend;

As just and right - eous is thy name, From trou - ble set me free.
Be thou my rock and fort - ress near, My help in time of need.
Do thou me lead for thy name's sake, And guide me in thy way.
Je - ho - vah, God of truth, to me Thou didst re - demp - tion send.

No. 36. WITH SONGS I'LL THEE EXTOL.

Ps. 30th, 1, 2, 5. 7s &6s.

J. C. Macy.

1 O Lord, by thee de - liv - ered, With songs I'll thee ex - tol: No en - 'my hast thou
2 His ho - li - ness, re - mem-ber, Ye saints give thanks and praise; A mo-ment lasts his
3 And now to joy-ous danc-ing My sor - row thou hast turned; And gird - ed me with

suf - fered To glo - ry o'er my fall. I cried to thee, Je - ho - vah, Thou
an - ger, His fa - vor crowns our days. For sor - row, like a pil - grim, May
glad - ness, Who had in sack cloth mourned; That un - to thee my glo - ry May

didst me heal and save; From death thou didst de - liv - er, And ran-som from the grave.
so-journ for a night, But joy the heart shall glad den, When dawns the morn-ing light.
cease-less praise ac-cord; For - ev - er I will ren - der Thanksgiving to the Lord.

No. 37. MERIBAH.

Ps. 31st, 18, 19. C. P. M.

Moderato.

1 O let Je-ho - vah bless-ed be, Who showed his wond'rous love to me
2 O love the Lord all that him serve, For he the faith-ful shall pre - serve,

In cit - y for - ti - fied; "Cut off from thee;" I said in fear,
And all the proud re - ward. Be of good cour-age; he with strength

Yet thou my suppliant voice didst hear, When un - to thee I cried.
Will fill your steadfast hearts at length, All ye who trust the Lord.

No. 38. I LOVE TO TELL THE STORY.

Ps. 32d, I, 2, 4-7. 7s & 6s.   By per. W. G. Fisher.

1 How blest the man whose tres - pass Hath free-ly pardoned been ; To whom the Lord hath
2 For this shall all the god - ly In prayer to thee a - bound ; In sea-sons they shall

giv - en   A   cov - er-ing for   sin   How blest to whom im - pu - ted   His
seek thee When thou art to be found. Great floods of wa - ter sure - ly   To

guilt no more shall   be :   The man in whom his spir - it From all de - ceit is free.
them shall not come nigh :   To thee, O Lord, my ref - uge And hid - ing place, I   fly.

My   tres - pass I   acknowledged,   Nor hid   my sin from   thee ;
From troub - les that   sur - round me Thou shalt   my soul keep   free ;

I   said, I'll make con - fes - sion ; Then thou for - gav - est   me.
With   songs of thy   sal - va - tion Thou shalt en - com - pass   me.

No. 39. TRUST IN GOD.

Ps. 37th, 3-6.   C. M.   F. Manford Clark.

1 Set thou thy trust up - on   the Lord, And be thou do ing good ; And   so thou in the
2 And like the morning light   he shall Thy righteousness dis-play ; And   he thy judgment

land shalt dwell, And ver - i - ly have food De - light thy - self in God ; he'll give Thy
shall bring forth Like noon-tide of the day. Rest in the Lord, in patience wait, Nor

heart's de - sire to thee. Thy way to God com-mit, him trust, It bring to pass shall he.
for the wicked fret. Who pros-per - ing in his evil way, Success in sin doth get.

No. 40. FEAR THE LORD.

Ps. 33d, 7, 9-11. C. M.

By per. P. J. Sprague.

1 The Lord to naught the coun - sel brings Which hea - then na - tions take;
2 The coun - sel of Je - ho - vah stands For - ev - er firm and sure;
3 That na - tion bless - ed is whose God Je - ho - vah is a - lone;

And what the peo - ple have de - vised Of no ef - fect doth make.
And of his heart the pur - po - ses From age to age en - dure.
The peo - ple bless - ed are whom he Hath chos - en for his own.

CHORUS.

Let earth and all that live there - in With rev'rence fear the Lord;

Let all the world's in - hab - i - tants dread him with one ac - cord.

No. 41. CHILDREN, COME.

Ps. 34th, 7, 9, 11. C. M.

P. J. Sprague.

1 O chil-dren, hith-er do ye come, And un-to me give ear;
2 De-part from ill, do good, seek peace, Pur-sue it ear-nest-ly.
3 The right-eous cry un-to the Lord, He un-to them gives ear;

I shall you teach to un-der-stand How ye the Lord should fear.
God's eyes are on the just, his ears Are o-pen to their cry.
And they out of their trou-bles all By him de-liv-ered are.

CHORUS.

Chil-dren, come, Hith-er'come,

Chil-dren, come, Hith-er come, And un-to me give ear;

I shall you teach to un-der-stand, How ye the Lord should fear.

No. 42. LYRA.

Ps. 36th, 5-8. C. M.

By per. GEO. F. ROOT.

1 Thy mer-cy, Lord, is in the heavens; Thy truth doth reach the clouds;
2 Lord, thou pre-serv-est man and beast. How prec-ious is thy grace;
3 They with the fat-ness of thy house Shall be well sat-is-fied;
4 Be-cause of life the foun-tain pure Re-mains a-lone with thee;

Thy jus-tice is like moun-tains great; Thy judg-ments deep as floods.
Therefore in sha-dow of thy wings Men's sons their trust shall place.
From riv-ers of thy pleas-ures thou Wilt drink to them pro-vide.
And in that pur-est light of thine, We clear-ly light shall see.

No. 43. IN THEE I'M TRUSTING.

Ps. 38th, 10-13. 8s & 7s.

REV. D. A. DUFF.

1 Lord, my God, in thee I'm trust-ing, Thou wilt hear me when I call:
2 Rea-dy now to halt and stum-ble, Griefs be-fore me still have been.
3 Great in pow-er, life and num-ber, Bit-ter foes have me with-stood,

Hear, lest they a-gainst me boast-ing, Joy and tri-umph when I fall.
I'll con-fess with spir-it hum-ble, And be sor-ry for my sin.
E-vil they for kind-ness ren-der, Hat-ing me for do-ing good.

CHORUS.

Lord, my God, do not for-sake me, Dis-tant from me nev-er be;

To my Sa-viour I be-take me; Has-ten, Lord, give help to me.

No. 44. AYLESBURY.

Ps. 39th, 8-11. S. M.

HARVEY CAMP.

1 As dumb, I si-lent stand, Be-cause this work is thine;
2 Re-bukes for sin con-sume, And chas-ten man with pain;
3 Je-ho-vah, hear my prayers, And an-swer my re-quest;
4 I am a stran-ger here, De-pend-ent on thy grace;

Re-move from me thy chastening hand, Be-neath thy stroke I pine.
Like moths they waste his beau-ty's bloom: Lo, ev-ery man is vain.
Turn not in si-lence from my tears, But give the mourn-er rest.
A pil-grim, as my fath-ers were, With no a-bid-ing place.

No. 45. WAITING PATIENTLY.

Ps. 40th, 1-6. C. M.   (From "Good Will," by per.)   W. I. HARTSHORN.

1 I wait - ed for the Lord my God, And pa - tiently did bear;
2 He put a new song in my mouth, Our God to mag - ni - fy;
3 O Lord, my God, how ma - ny are The won - ders thou hast done?

At length to me he did incline My voice and cry to hear.
Ma - ny shall see it, and shall fear, And on the Lord re - ly.
Thy gracious thoughts to us a - bove All oth - er thoughts are gone.

He took me from a fear - ful pit, And from the mi - ry clay,
O bless - ed is the man whose trust Up - on the Lord re - lies;
To thee no one can them express; If I would them de - clare—

Up - on a rock he set my feet, Es - tab - lish - ing my way.
Re - spect - ing not the proud, nor such As turn a - side to lies.
If I would speak of them, they more Than can be numbered are.

No. 46. REST.

Ps. 41st, 1-3. L. M.   By per. W. B. BRADBURY.

1 Blest he who wise - ly helps the poor, In trou - ble he shall help se - cure;
2 Thou wilt not give him to the will Of foes that seek to do him ill.
3 On him thou wilt com - pas - sion take, And all his bed in sick - ness make.

The Lord shall keep him, he shall live, And blessing on the earth re - ceive.
When laid up - on the bed of pain, The Lord with strength will him sus - tain.
I said, Lord, pit - y, heal thou me, Because I have of - fend - ed thee.

No. 47. LORD, HASTEN TO MY AID.

Ps. 40th, 13-15, 18, 19. C. M.

D. C. JOHN.

1 Thy ten-der mer-cies, Lord, from me O do thou not re-strain;
2 For ills past reck'ning com-pass me, And my in-i-qui-ties
3 They more than hairs are on my head; Thence is my heart dis-mayed.
4 In thee let all be glad, and joy Who seek-ing thee a-bide;

Thy lov-ing-kind-ness and thy truth, Let them me still main-tain.
Such hold up-on me tak-en have, I can-not lift my eyes:
Be pleased, O Lord, to res-cue me; Lord, has-ten to my aid.
Who thy sal-va-tion love, say still, The Lord be mag-ni-fied.

Duet.

I poor and need-y am, but yet The Lord of me takes thought:

Full.

Thou art my Sa-viour and my help; My God, O tar-ry not.

Ps. 42d, 1-4. 8s & 4s.

No. 48. TOY.

R. S. TAYLOR.

1 As pants the hart for cool-ing flood, So pants my soul, O liv-ing God, To taste thy grace.
2 Tears day and night have been my bread, Whilst, "Where is now thy God?" is said, By foes to me.
3 With numbers gathered from abroad I went to seek the house of God, With joy and praise.
4 O thou my soul, why so depressed? Why thus with vexing thoughts oppressed? On God rely;

When un-to thee shall I draw near? O when within thy courts appear, And see thy face?
I call these things to mind with grief. My soul I then, to find re-lief, Pour out to thee.
I ever joined with true de-light The multitude which kept aright The ho-ly days.
For I shall yet behold his face; My God, who helps me by his grace, I'll mag-ni-fy.

No. 49. IN GOD WE BOAST.

Ps. 44th, 1, 2, 4. IIs.

FRANK M. DAVIS.

1 O God, we have heard, and our fa-thers have taught The works which of old, in their
2 They gained not the land by the edge of the sword, Their own arm to them could no

day, thou hadst wrought. The na-tions were crushed, and ex-pelled by thy hand, Cast
safe-ty af-ford; But by thy right hand, and the light of thy face, The

CHORUS.

out that thy peo-ple might dwell in their land.
strength of thy arm, and be-cause of thy grace. } No trust will I place in my

bow to de-fend, Nor yet on my sword for my safe-ty de-pend. In

God who has saved us and put them to shame, We boast all the day, ever praising his name.

No. 50. KEOKUK.

Ps. 45th, 13-17. C. M.

By per. W. B. BRADBURY.

1 Be-hold, the daugh-ter of the King All glori-ous is with-in;
2 She shall be brought be-fore the King In robes with nee-dle wrought;
3 With glad-ness and re-joic-ings great Thou all of them wilt bring;
4 In-stead of those thy fath-ers dear, Thy chil-dren thou shalt take,
5 Thy name re-mem-bered I will make Through a-ges all to be;

And with em-broid-er-ies of gold Her gar-ments wrought have been;
Her fel-low-vir-gins fol-low-ing Shall un-to thee be brought;
And they to-geth-er en-ter shall The pal-ace of the King;
And in all pla-ces of the earth Them no-ble prin-ces make;
The peo-ple there-fore ev-er-more Shall prais-es give to thee;

And with em-broid-er-ies of gold Her garments wrought have been.
Her fel-low-vir-gins fol-low-ing Shall un-to thee be brought.
And they to-geth-er en-ter shall The pal-ace of the King.
And in all pla-ces of the earth Them no-ble prin-ces make.
The peo-ple there-fore ev-er-more Shall prais-es give to thee.

Ps. 46th. 1-4. C. M. **No. 51. GOD OUR REFUGE.** By per. WM. F. SHERWIN.

1 God is our ref-uge and our strength, In straits a pres-ent aid;
2 A riv-er is whose streams make glad The cit-y of our God;

And there-fore tho' the earth re-move, We will not be a-fraid.
The ho-ly place wherein the Lord Most High has his a-bode.

Though hills a-midst the seas be cast, be cast, Though wa-ters roar-ing make, roaring make,
God in the midst of her doth dwell, doth dwell, And noth-ing shall her move, shall her move;

And trou-bled be; yea, tho' the hills, tho' the hills, By swell-ing seas do shake.
God al-so ve-ry ear-ly will, ear-ly will, To her a help-er prove.

No. 52. THE PENITENT.

Ps. 43d. 2-5. 8s & 7s.   From "BRIGHT JEWELS," by per. BIGLOW & MAIN.   CHESTER G. ALLEN.

1 God, my rock, my strength sus - tain - ing, Why cast off my soul dis-
2 There thine al - tar, Lord, sur - round - ing, God, my God, my bound-less

tress'd? Why am I in grief com - plain - ing, By the power of foes op-
joy, Harp and voice a - loud re - sound - ing, Praise shall all my powers em-

press'd? Now thy light and truth forth send - ing, Let them lead and guide me
ploy. Why, my soul, cast down and griev - ing? Why with - in me such dis-

still, Guide me to thy house as - cend - ing, Lead me to thy ho - ly hill.
tress? Hope in God, his help re - ceiv - ing, God my life I yet shall bless.

Ps. 45th, 3-7   S. M.   ## No. 53. ST. THOMAS.   A. WILLIAMS.

Spirited.

1 More fair than sons of men; Grace in thy lips doth flow:
2 Thy sword gird on thy thigh, Thou that art great in might:
3 For meek - ness, truth, and right, Ride pros - perous - ly in state;
4 Thy shafts shall pierce the hearts Of those that hate the King;
5 Thy roy - al seat, O Lord, For - ev - er shall re - main;

And there - fore bless-ings ev - er - more On thee doth God be - stow.
Ap - pear in dread ful ma - jes - ty, And in thy glo - ry bright.
And thy right hand shall teach to thee Things ter - ri - ble and great.
And un - der thy do - min - ion thou The peo - ple down shall bring.
The scep - tre of thy king - dom doth All right - eous - ness main - tain.

No. 54. THE RIVER FLOWS.

Ps. 46th, 2-4. 8s & 6s.

By per. REV. M. F. McKIRAHAN.

1 A riv - er flows whose wa - ters clear, The cit - y of our God make glad,
2 The na - tions rage, the kingdoms shake, His voice goes forth, earth melts a - way,
3 To earth's re - mot - est bounds he turns Wars in - to peace : he breaks the bow ;

The ho - ly tab - er - na - cles, where The High - est One his dwell-ing made.
The Lord of hosts our part doth take, And Ja - cob's God is shield and stay.
He cuts the spear, the char - iot burns, That I am God, be still and know ;

In midst of her hath God, Es - tablished his a - bode ; No trou - ble can her
Come, then, let all draw near, And view with ho - ly fear The works sur-pass-ing
A - mong the heath-en I Will be ex - alt - ed high ; On earth su-preme. The

move, For God her help will prove, When morning light dawns from a - bove.
thought Je-ho-vah's arm hath wrought, What ru-ins he on earth hath brought.
Lord Of hosts doth aid af - ford, And Ja - cob's God is shield and sword.

Ps. 47th, 1-5. S. M.

No. 55. CONVERSE.

ANTON GERSBACH.

1 All na-tions clap your hands, Let shouts of tri - umph ring, For dread - ful o - ver
2 He'll quell the peo-ple's rage, And na - tions will de - stroy ; For us will choose our
3 With shouts ascends our King, With trum-pets' stir-ring call ; Praise, praise ye God, his
4 O sing in joy - ful strains, In songs his truth make known ; God o - ver all the
5 The heirs of gen - tile thrones With Abr'am's chil-dren meet. The shields of earth Je-

all the lands The Lord Most High is King, The Lord Most High is King.
her - i - tage, His chos - en Ja - cob's joy, His chos - en Ja - cob's joy.
prais - es sing, For God is Lord of all, For God is Lord of all.
na - tions reigns, High on his ho - ly throne, High on his ho - ly throne.
ho - vah owns Ex - alt - ed is his seat, Ex - alt - ed is his seat.

34

No. 56. THE LORD IS GREAT.

Ps. 48th, 1, 2, 7-9. S. M.

Rev. M. F. McKibahan.

1 The Lord our God is great, And great-ly to be praised, With-in his ci - ty
2 The joy of all the earth, The walls of Zi - on rise Most beau-ti - ful, and
3 With in thy tem - ple, Lord, In that most ho - ly place, We on thy lov - ing-
4 Ac - cord - ing to thy name Through all the earth's thy praise ; And ev' - ry work of

CHORUS.

where his throne Is on Mount Zi - on raised.)
on the north The great King's ci - ty lies.)
kindness thought, And wonders of thy grace. } Let Zi - on now re - joice, And
thy right hand Thy righteousness dis - plays.)

Judah's daughters sing ; Let them with joy ful ness proclaim The judgments of their King.

No. 57. LET ZION REJOICE.

Ps. 48th, 1-3. H. M.

Rev. D. A. Duff.

1 Within thy tem - ple, Lord, We on thy mer - cies dwell ; As is thy name a-
2 Let Zi - on Mount rejoice, Let Ju - dah's daughters praise The Lord with cheer-ful
3 The towers of Zi - on tell, Her pal - a - ces sur - vey, Mark all her bul-warks

Thy praise - - es sound thro'
Go round the walls on
This God for - ev - - er

dored, So let thy praise ex - cel ; Thy prais-es sound thro' ev' - ry land, Thy
voice, For judg - ment he displays ; Go round the walls on Zi - on's Mount, Go
well, And to your chil - dren say: This God for - ev - er shall a - bide, This

ev - 'ry land.
Zi - on's Mount.
shall a - bide.

prais - es sound thro' ev' - ry land, And right thy scep - tre shall command.
round the walls on Zi - on's Mount, Go round her splen - dors to re - count.
God for - ev - er shall a - bide, Ev'n un - to death our God and guide.

Ps. 50th, 3-6. S. M. No. 58. SILVER STREET. I. Smith.

1 Our God shall sure - ly come, Keep si - lence shall not he:
2 Then to the heav - ens high He from a - bove shall call,
3 To - geth - er let my saints He gath - ered un - to me.
4 The heav - ens then shall show His right - eous - ness a - broad.

Be - fore him fire shall waste, great storms Shall round a - bout him be.
And like - wise to the earth that he May judge his peo - ple all.
Those that by sac - ri - fice have made A cov - e - nant with me.
Be - cause the Lord him - self is judge; Yea, none is judge but God.

Ps. 51st. 1, 4, 5. 7s. No. 59. WHITER THAN SNOW. W. T. Wiley.

1 Lord, to me com - pas - sion show, As thy ten - der mer - cies flow;
2 Wash from ev' - ry guil - ty stain, Cleanse with hys - sop, make me clean;
3 From my sins hide thou thy face, Blot them out in thy rich grace;

In thy vast and boundless grace, My trans - gress - ions all e - rase;
Then from all pol - lu - tion free, Whit - er than the snow I'll be.
Free my heart, O God, from sin, Spir - it right re - new with - in.

Wash me whol - ly from my sins, Cleanse me from my guil - ty stains,
Let me hear joy's cheering tones, Mak - ing glad these brok - en bones,
Cast me not a - way from thee, Nor thy Spir - it take from me,

Wash me whol - ly from my sins, Cleanse me from my guil - ty stains,
Let me hear joy's cheering tones, Mak - ing glad these brok en bones.
Cast me not a - way from thee, Nor thy Spir - it take from me.

No. 60. ROCK OF AGES.

Ps. 51st, 7-9. 7s.

DR. HASTINGS.

1 Freed from guilt, my tongue shall raise Songs thy right - eous-ness to praise;
2 Sac - ri - fice, or burnt - off' - ring, Can to thee no pleas-ure bring;
3 Zi - on fa - vor in thy grace, Yea, Je - rus' - lem's ramparts raise,

O - pen thou my lips, O Lord, Then my mouth shall praise ac - cord;
But a spir - it crushed for sin, Con - trite, bro - ken heart with - in,
Then shall sac - ri - fi - ces right, Whole burnt-off' - rings thee de - light;

Sac - ri - fice thou wilt not take, Else would I the off' - ring make.
Thine ac - cept - ed sac - ri - fice, Thou, O God, wilt not de - spise.
So shall men, their vows to pay, Vic - tims on thine al - tar lay.

No. 61. GIVE EAR.

Ps. 61st, 1-4. C. M.

C. F. POLLOCK.

1 O God, give ear un - to my cry, And to my prayer at - tend. From th' utmost corner
2 And when my heart is overwhelm'd, And in per-plex-i-ty, Do thou me lead un-
3 For thou hast for my ref - uge been A shel - ter by thy power; And for de - fense a-
4 With-in thy tab - er - na - cle I For - ev - er will a - bide; And un - der cov-ert

CHORUS.

of the land My cry to thee I'll send.
to the Rock That high-er is than I.   Give ear,   give ear,
gainst my foes Thou hast been my strong tower.
of thy wings With con - fi - dence will hide.

O God, give ear un - to my cry,

And to my prayer at - tend; Give ear, give ear, My cry to thee I'll send.

O God, give ear un - to my cry.

No. 62. LUTHER.

Ps. 53d, 1-3, 7. S. M.
Vigoroso.
HASTINGS.

1 That there is not a God, Fools in their hearts conclude ; Cor - rupt they
2 Up - on the sons of men God looked from hea-ven abroad, To see if
3 To - geth - er all are vile, They all a - side are gone ; And there is
4 From Zi - on, Lord, give help, And back thy cap - tives bring ; Then Ja - cob

dim.

are, their works are vile, Not one of them doth good, Not one of them doth good.
a - ny un - derstood, If a - ny sought for God, If a - ny sought for God.
none that do - eth good, No, not so much as one, No not so much as one.
shall ex - ult with joy, And Is - ra - el shall sing, And Is - ra - el shall sing.

No. 63. SALVATION.

Ps. 54th, 1-4. S. M.
By per. W. T. WILEY.

1 Save by thy name, O Lord, In power my judge ap - pear ;
2 My help - er is the Lord, With those who me de - fend ;

My ear - nest prayer do thou re - gard, And to my voice give ear.
With ill he shall my foes re - ward, On them de - struc-tion send.

For foes a - gainst me rise, Op - press - ors seek my soul ; ·
I'll free - will off' - rings bring, And sac - ri - fice with joy,

They set not God be - fore their eyes, Nor own his just con - trol.
Thy name is good ; its praise to sing My tongue I will em - ploy.

No. 64. SILVERTON.

Ps. 56th, 3, 8, 9. C. M.

1 When I'm a-fraid I'll trust in thee: In God I'll praise his word;
2 I will not fear what man can do; For I on God re - ly.
3 From death thou hast me saved; my feet Do thou from falls keep free:

I will not fear what flesh can do, My trust is in the Lord.
Thy vows up-on me are, O God: To thee give praise will I.
So in the light of those who live I'll walk, O Lord, with thee.

No. 65. APHEKA.

Ps. 57th, 6, 8-10. C. M.

1 Be thou ex - alt - ed ve - ry high A - bove the heavens, O God; And
2 I'll praise thee with the peo - ple, Lord, With na - tions sing will I; For

let thy glo - ry be advanced O'er all the earth a - broad. My heart, O God, is
great to heaven thy mer - cy is, Thy truth is to the sky. A - bove the heav - ens

fixed, is fixed; To thee I'll sing, and praise; A - wake my glo - ry,
high, O God, Do thou ex - alt - ed be; And let thy glo - ry

lute, and harp; My - self I'll ear - ly raise, My - self I'll ear - ly raise.
be ad-vanced A - bove both land and sea, A - bove both land and sea.

No. 66. THERE IS A FOUNTAIN.

Ps. 62d, 1, 2, 7, 8. C. M.

WESTERN MELODY.

1 My soul with ex - pec - ta - tion doth De - pend on God in - deed;
2 In God a - lone my glo - ry is, And my sal - va - tion sure;
3 On him, ye peo - ple, ev - er - more With con - fi - dence re - ly;

My strength and my sal - va - tion do From him a - lone pro - ceed.
My rock of strength is in the Lord, My ref - uge most se - cure.
Be - fore him pour ye out your heart; God is our ref - uge high.

REFRAIN.

He on - ly my sal - va - tion is, And my strong rock is he;

He on - ly is my sure de - fence; And moved I shall not be.

No. 67. ALL LANDS TO GOD.

Ps. 66th, 1, 2, 3, 7. C. M.

1 All lands to God, in joy - ful sounds, A - loft your voi - ces raise; Sing
2 Say ye to God, how ter - ri - ble In all thy works art thou! Thro'
3 And all the earth shall wor - ship thee, They shall thy praise pro - claim; With
4 O all ye peo - ple, bless our God, A - loud pro - claim his praise, Who

forth the honor of his name And glo - rious make his praise, And glorious make his praise.
thy great pow'r thy foes to thee Shall be constrained to bow, Shall be constrained to bow.
cheerful heart aloud they shall Sing to thy ho - ly name, Sing to thy ho - ly name.
safe - ly holds our soul in life, Our foot from slid - ing stays, Our foot from slid - ing stays.

No. 68. ARIEL.

Ps. 63d, 1-3.   C. P. M.

Dr. L. Mason.

cres.

1 Thou art my God, O God Most High, And
2 I long as in the times of old, Thy
3 Thus will I bless thee while I live, And

ear - ly seek thy face will I; My soul doth thirst for thee.
power and glo - ry to be - hold With - in thy ho - ly place;
with up - lift - ed hands will give Praise to thy ho - ly name.

My spir - it thirsts to taste thy grace, My flesh longs in this
Be - cause to me thy won - drous love Than life it - self doth
As when with fat - ness well sup - plied, So shall my soul be

bar - ren place In which no wa - ters be, In which no wa - ters be.
dear - er prove, My lips shall praise thy grace, My lips shall praise thy grace.
sat is - fied, My mouth shall praise pro - claim, My mouth shall praise pro - claim.

No. 69. MARSELLA.

Ps. 66th, 12-14.   C. M.

By per. Wm. Martin.

1 All that fear God, come, hear, I'll tell What he did for my
2 If in my heart I sin re - gard, Je - ho - vah will not
3 O let the Lord, our gra - cious God, For - ev - er bless - ed

soul. I with my mouth cried un - to him, My tongue did him ex - tol.
hear; But sure - ly God hath heard my voice, At - tend - ing to my prayer.
be, Who hath not turned my prayer from him, Nor yet his grace from me.

Ps. 65th, 1-6. 7s & 6s.

C. E. POLLOCK.

1 Praise waits for thee in Zi - on, To thee vows paid shall be; O thou of prayer the
2 Blest he whom thou hast cho - sen, And un - to thee brought nigh; Who hath for ha - bi-
3 O God of our sal - va - tion, We plead with thee in prayer; Thy righteousness makes

hear - er, All flesh shall come to thee. In - i - qui - ties a-gainst me Pre-
ta - tion The courts of God Most High. We shall in rich a-bun-dance Be
ans - wer By things which fear ful are. Of earth the ends re - mo - test, And

vail from day to day; But as for our transgressions, Them shalt thou purge a-way.
sat - is - fied with grace, And filled with all the good-ness Of thy most ho - ly place.
those a - far at sea, These all, O Lord, are plac-ing Their con - fi - dence in thee.

Ps. 65th, 9-12. 7s & 6s.

No. 71. WEBB.

G. J. WEBB.

1 Thy vis - it brings the show - ers, Thy floods en-rich the field: Thy bless-ing so pro-
2 The year is crown'd with goodness, Thy paths drop fat-ness round; The lit - tle hills and

vides it, That earth our food shall yield. Thou wa - ter - est her rid - ges, Her
pas - tures With joy-ful-ness re - sound. The fields with flocks are cov - ered, The

fur-rows down are pressed, With show-ers they are soft-ened, Her spring by thee is blest.
vales with corn are clad; They shout, yea, they are sing - ing, For thou hast made them glad.

No. 72. VARINA.

Ps. 68th, 1, 3-5. C.M.

Arr. by Geo. F. Root.

1 { Let God a - rise, and scat - tered far Let all his en' - mies be ; }
{ And let all those who do him hate Be - fore his pres - ence flee. }
2 { O sing to God and praise his name ; Ex - tol him with your voice, }
{ That rides on heav'n by his name JAH ; Be - fore his face re - joice. }

But let the right - eous all be glad ; Re - joice be - fore God's sight ;
Be - cause the Lord a fath - er is To chil - dren fath - er - less ;

Let them ex - ult ex - ceed - ing - ly, And joy with all their might.
He is the wid - ow's judge, with - in His place of ho - li - ness.

No. 73. THE ASCENDED SAVIOUR.

Ps. 68th, 17-20. 7s & 6s.

Dr. L. Mason.

1 Thou hast, O Lord, with glo - ry As - cend - ed up a - gain, And captive led cap -
2 Blest be the Lord Je - ho - vah, Of our sal - va - tion God, Who us with blessings

tiv - ity Tri - umphant in thy train. To thee have gifts been grant - ed For
dai - ly A - bun - dant - ly doth load. He is the Lord, the Sa - viour, Who

men who did re - bel, That so the Lord Je - ho - vah In midst of them might dwell.
is our God most High : And with the Lord Je - ho - vah From death the is - sues lie.

No. 74. BEALOTH.

Ps. 67th, 1-4. S. M.

1 Lord, bless, and pi - ty us, Shine on us with thy face: That
2 Thou'lt just - ly peo - ple judge; On earth rule na - tions all. Let

earth thy way, and na - tions all May know thy sav - ing grace. Let
peo - ple praise thee, Lord; let them Praise thee, both great and small. The

peo - ple praise thee, Lord, Let peo - ple all thee praise: O
earth her fruit shall yield; Our God shall bless - ing send. God

let the na - tions all be glad, In songs their voi - ces raise.
will us bless; men shall him fear To earth's re - mot - est end.

No. 75. DOWNS.

Ps. 71st, 1-4. C. M.

1 O Lord, my hope and con - fi - dence Are placed a - lone in thee;
2 And let me, in thy right - eous - ness, From thee de - liv - rance have;
3 Be thou my dwell - ing rock, to which I ev - er may re - sort:
4 Free me, my God, from wick - ed hands, Hands cru - el and un - just;

Then let me ev - er - more be kept From all con - fu - sion free.
O res - cue me, in - cline thine ear To hear me, and me save.
Thou my sal - va - tion hast or - dained; Thou art my rock and fort.
For thou, O Lord God, art my hope, And from my youth my trust.

No. 76. SALEM. T. E. PERKINS.

1 Through all the earth, ye king - doms, Sing un - to God the
2 Strength un - to God at - trib - ute, His glor - ious ma - jes -

King; Sing prais - es to Je - ho - vah, His praise, O do ye
ty O'er Isr' - el is, his pow - er Is in the heav - ens

sing. He rides on heaven of heav - ens, Which he of old did
high. Thou, from thy house art dread - ful; Isr' - el's own God is

found; Lo, when his voice is ut - tered His words in might a - bound.
he, Who gives strength to his peo - ple, O let God bless - ed be.

No. 77. HIDE NOT THY FACE.

1 Lord, hear me, for thy love And kind - ness is most good; O
2 Hide not thy face from me, I'm trou - bled, soon at - tend, Draw
3 Thou my re - proach dost know, My shame and my dis - grace; Those
4 Re - proach hath broke my heart; I'm full of grief; for one To
5 They al - so gave me gall, They gave it for my meat; They

turn, and man - i - fest to me Thy mer - cies' mul - ti - tude.
near, thy ser - vant's soul re - deem, Me from my foes de - fend.
that are en - e - mies to me Are all be - fore thy face.
pi - ty me I looked in vain, All com - fort - ers were gone.
gave me vin - e - gar to drink, What time my thirst was great.

No. 78. ZERAH.

Ps. 72d, 6-9. C.M.
Arr. from HANDEL by DR. L. MASON.

1 His large and great do - min - ion shall From sea to sea ex - tend;
2 They in the wil - der - ness that dwell Bow down be - fore him must;
3 The Kings of Tars - hish, and the isles, To him shall pre-sents bring;
9 Yea, all the migh - ty kings on earth Be fore him down shall fall;

It from the riv - er shall reach forth To earth's re - mo - test end.
And they that are his en - e - mies Shall lick the ve - ry dust.
And un - to him shall of - fer gifts She - ba's and Se - ba's king.
And all the na - tions of the world Do ser - vice to him shall.

It from the riv - er shall reach forth To earth's re - mo - test end.
And they that are his en - e - mies Shall lick the ve - ry dust.
And un - to him shall of - fer gifts She - ba's and Se - ba's king.
And all the na - tions of the world Do ser - vice to him shall.

No. 79. CORONATION.

Ps. 72d, 17, 18. C.M.
OLIVER HOLDEN.

1 Now bless - ed be Je - ho - vah, God, The God of Is - ra - el,
2 And bless - ed be his glo - rious name To all e - ter - ni - ty:

Who on - ly do - eth won - drous works, In glo - ry that ex - cel.
The whole earth let his glo - ry fill, A - men, so let it be.

Who on - ly do - eth won - drous works, In glo - ry that ex - cel.
The whole earth let his glo - ry fill, A - men, so let it be.

No. 80. MAKE HASTE.

C. E. Pollock.

1 Make haste, O my God, to de - liv-er I pray, O Lord to my suc-cor make haste:
2 Let all them that seek thee be glad and re-joice, And who thy sal - va-tion would see;
3 But I, poor and nee - dy, still trust in thy word; Make haste to the res-cue, I pray;

Let them be confounded who seek me to slay And in their own fol-ly dis - graced.
In anthems of praise let them lift up the voice, And con-stant-ly mag-ni-fy thee.
My help-er thou art, and my Saviour, O Lord, No long-er thy com-ing de - lay.

CHORUS.

Make haste, Make haste, Make haste to the res-cue I pray;

Make haste, Make haste,

My help-er thou art, and my Saviour, O Lord, No lon-ger thy coming de - lay.

No. 81. THE LORD ONLY.

Ps. 73d, 19-23. C. M.

W. S. Pitts, by per.

1 O whom have I in heav-ens high, But thee, O Lord a - lone?
2 My flesh and heart do faint and fail, But God my heart sus - tains;
3 For lo, they that are far from thee, For - ev - er per - ish shall;
4 But sure - ly it is good for me That I draw near to God:

And in the earth whom I de - sire, Be - sides thee there is none.
The strength and por - tion of my heart, He ev - er - more re - mains.
And as for those who from thee stray, Thou hast de-stroyed them all.
In God I trust, that all thy works, I may de - clare a - broad.

CHORUS.

With thy good counsel while I live, while I live, Thou wilt me safe-ly guide;

And in-to glo-ry af-ter-ward Re-ceive me to a-bide, to a-bide.

Ps. 77th, 1-3, 5. L. M.

No. 82. I CRIED TO GOD.

W. S. MARSHALL.

1 I cried to God, I cried, he heard; In day of grief I sought the Lord;
2 I thought of God, and was distressed; Complained, yet trou-ble round me pressed;
3 The days of old I called to mind, The an-cient years when God was kind;

All night with hands stretched out I wept, My soul no com-fort would ac-cept.
Thou hold-est, Lord, my eyes a-wake; So great my grief I can-not speak.
I called to mind my song by night, My mus-ing spir-it sought for light.

CHORUS.

Hath God for-got-ten to be kind? His ten-der love in wrath con-fined?

My weak-ness this, yet faith doth stand Re-call-ing years of God's right hand.

48

No. 83. I HEAR THY VOICE.

Ps. 79th. 8, 9, 11, 13. S. M.   By per. Ph. Phillips.

1 Mind not our for-mer sins; Thy ten-der mer-cies show; O
2 For thy name's glo-ry help, Who hast our Sa-viour been; De-
3 In mer-cy, Lord, draw near, And hear the pris'-ner's sigh; Pre-

let them vis-it us with speed, We are brought ve-ry low.
liv-er us for thy name's sake, And purge a-way our sin.
serve those in thy migh-ty power That are con-demned to die.

CHORUS.

So we thy cho-sen flock Will ev-er praise thy name; With

thank-ful hearts to a-ges all Thy praise we will pro-claim.

No. 84. ROTHWELL.

Ps. 76th, 5-7. L. M.   English.
Firm and Spirited.

1 From heav'n Jehovah judgment gave; The trembling earth stood still and fear'd, When all the meek on
2 The wrath of man thee praise shall bring, Remaining wrath thy hand shall stay. Vow to the Lord your
3 Let all a-round their pres-ents bring To him whom all the world should fear: He cuts off princes;

earth to save, For righteous judg-ment God appeared, For righteous judg-ment God ap-peared.
God and King, Be faith-ful all your vows to pay, Be faith-ful all your vows to pay.
God the King Shall dreadful to earth's kings ap-pear, Shall dreadful to earth's kings ap-pear.

No. 85. JESUS' CROSS.

Ps. 88th, 1-6. 8s & 7s.   L. O. EMERSON.

1 O thou God of my sal - va - tion, Day and night I cried to thee;
2 Free to sleep in death's dark cham - ber, Like the slain with - in the grave;
3 Friendship's ties by thee are bro - ken, Friends are ban - ished from my sight;

Hear my hum - ble sup - pli - ca - tion, Quick - ly bow thine ear to me.
Whom thou dost no more re - mem - ber, Whom thy hand no more shall save.
Scorned by them, my name is spok - en; Closed on me is sor - row's night.

Filled with grief, my soul is sigh - ing, To the grave my life draws near,
In the pit thy hand has laid me, In the dark - ness and in deeps;
Mourns my eye, my pow - ers lan - guish, Sore af - flic - tion press - es me;

Num - bered now a - mong the dy - ing; Like one help - less I ap - pear.
Sore - ly has thy wrath dismayed me; O'er my soul af - flic - tion sweeps.
Lord, I cry to thee in an - guish, Dai - ly stretch my hand to thee.

No. 86. CLARK.

Ps. 89th, 15-18. C. M.   Arr. by R. B. ROBERTSON.

Ardito.

1 O great - ly bless'd the peo - ple are, The joy - ful sound that know; In bright-ness of thy
2 They in thy name shall all the day Re - joice ex - ceed - ing - ly; And in thy right-eous-
3 Be-cause the glo - ry of their strength Doth on - ly stand in thee: And in thy fa - vor
4 For God is our de-fence; he will To us sal - va - tion bring: The Ho - ly One of

face, O Lord, They ev - er on shall go, They ev - er on shall go.
ness shall they Ex - alt - ed be on high, Ex - alt - ed be on high.
shall our horn And pow'r ex - alt - ed be, And pow'r ex - alt - ed be.
Is - ra - el Is our al - might - y King, Is our al - might - y King.

No. 87. O THOU SHEPHERD OF ISRAEL.

Ps. 80th, 1, 2, 10. 11s.

1 O thou who the Shep - herd of Is - ra - el art, Give ear to our pray'r, and thy
2 In E-phra-im's, Manasseh's and Ben-ja-min's sight, O come thou and save us: a-
3 No more shall we wan - der, delight-ing in shame; Re - vive us, O Lord; we will

fa - vor im - part; Thou lead - er of Jo - seph, thou
wake in thy might. O God, give us fa - vor, re -
call on thy name. O Lord God of hosts, us re -

guide of his way, Mid cher-u-bim dwell-ing, thy glo-ry dis-play.
store to thy grace; And then we shall live in the light of thy face.
store to thy grace, And then we shall live in the light of thy face.

No. 88. OSTEND.

Ps. 84th, 8-11. C. M.

By per. Dr. L. Mason.

1 Lord God of hosts, my pray - er hear; O Ja - cob's God, give ear.
2 For God the Lord's a sun and shield: He'll grace and glo - ry give;

See, God, our shield, look on the face Of thy an - oint - ed dear.
And no good thing will he with - hold From them that just - ly live.

For in thy courts one day ex - cels A thou - sand; ra - ther in
O thou that art the Lord of hosts, That man is tru - ly blest.

My God's house will I keep a door, Than dwell in tents of sin.
Who with un-shak-en con - fi-dence On thee a-lone doth rest.

No. 89. TURN US.

Ps. 85th, 1-3. L. P. M.

By per. Rev. D. A. Duff.

1 Lord, thou hast favor shown thy land, And brought back Jacob's captive band; Thy people's sins thou
2 Turn us, O God our Saviour, turn, Nor lon-ger let thine an ger burn. Wilt thou for-ev - er
3 O Lord, to us thy mer-cy show, And thy sal - va - tion now be-stow; We wait to hear what

par - doned hast, And all their guilt hast covered o'er, Removed from them thine
an - gry be? Through a - ges shall thy wrath survive! Wilt thou not us a-
God will say: Peace to his peo - ple he will speak, And to his saints, but

CHORUS.

an - ger sore, All thy fierce wrath behind thee cast.
gain re vive, That so we may re-joice in thee?   Turn us, turn us, O
let them seek No more in fol-ly's path to stray.

God, our Sa-viour, turn; Turn us, turn us, O God, our Saviour, turn.

No. 90. LORD GOD OF HOSTS, HOW LOVELY!

Ps. 84th, 1-4, 9.   7s & 6s.   Dr. J. B. Herbert.

1 Lord God of hosts, how love-ly The place where thou dost dwell! Thy
2 Be-hold the spar-row find-eth A house in which to rest, The

tab-er-na-cles ho-ly In pleas-ant-ness ex-cel. My soul is long-ing,
swal-low hath dis-cov-ered Where she may build her nest; And where, se-cure-ly

faint-ing, Je-ho-vah's courts to see; My heart and flesh are cry-ing,
shel-ter-d, Her young she forth may bring; So, Lord of hosts, thy al-tars

CHORUS.

O liv-ing God, for thee.)
I seek, my God, my King.)   One day ex-cels a thou-sand, If

spent thy courts within; I'll choose thy threshold ra-ther Than dwell in tents of sin.

No. 91. ALL GLORY TO GOD.

Ps. 86th, 6-11.   C. M.   By per. J. H. Tenney.

1 O Lord, a-mong the hea-then gods Like thee there is not one; Nor are there a-ny
2 All na-tions, Lord, whom thou hast made Shall come and praise proclaim; Be-fore thy face, they
3 Be-cause thou art ex-ceed-ing great, And works by thee are done, Which are to be ad-
4 Teach me thy way, and in thy truth, O Lord, then walk will I; U-nite my heart that
5 Be-cause thy mer-cy to-ward me In great-ness doth ex-cel; And thou de-liv-ered

O Lord, my God, with all my heart,

works, O Lord, Like those which thou hast done.
wor-ship shall, And glo-ri-fy thy name.
mired; and thou Art God thy-self a-lone.
I thy name May fear con-tin-ual-ly.
hast my soul Out from the low-est hell.

O Lord my God, with all my heart Thy

O Lord, my God, with all my heart

praise I will pro-claim; I will as-cribe for-ev-er-more All glo-ry to thy name.

I will as-cribe forever-more

I will as-cribe for-ev-er-more

No. 92. GOD'S FOUNDATION.

Ps. 87th, 1, 2, 4, 5. 7s.

By per. W. O. PERKINS.

1 God's foun-da-tion stands un-moved, On the high and ho-ly hills;
2 God the High-est by his might Will es-tab-lish her on earth;

Zi-on's gates by him are loved, More than tents where Ja-cob dwells.
God shall na-tions' re-cords write, "Count-ing these in her had birth."

O thou ci-ty of the Lord, Glo-rious things are said of thee;
Those on in-stru-ments that play, Shall with sin-gers joy-ful be;

Ba-by-lon, I will re-cord, Ra-hab, too, as know-ing me.
And with one ac-cord shall say, "All my springs are found in thee."

No. 93. WHY ME FORSAKE.

Ps. 88th, 7-12. 8s & 7s.

Cantabile.

W. IRVING HARTSHORN.

1 Shall the dead, to life re-turn-ing, Rise and sing thy won-ders, Lord,
2 But, O Lord, at dawn a-wak-ing, Prayer and cries I'll send to thee:
3 Flames of wrath are o'er me leap-ing Hor-rors great up-on me roll;

Shall the grave thy love be learn-ing, Death thy faith - ful ness re - cord?
Why, my God, my soul for-sak-ing, Hi-dest thou thy face from me?
Round they come like wa - ters sweep-ing, Dai - ly com - pass ing my soul.

Shall thy works and won-drous do-ing, Be pro-claimed in dark-ness deep?
All my days I've been af-flict-ed, Rea-dy from my youth to die;
Thou my dear - est friends hast banished, My com-pan - ions put to flight;

Right-eous-ness shall they be view-ing, Wrapt in cold ob-liv-ion's sleep?
I with suff - rings am dis-tract - ed, While thy ter - rors on me lie.
All ac-quain - tan-ces have vanished, Driv-en to the shades of night.

No. 94. UPTON.

Ps. 89th, 4, 5, 7. L. M.

By per. DR. L. MASON.

1 The wonders done by thee, O Lord, The heavens shall in praise re - cord;
2 For who in heav'n 'mid dwel-lers there, Can to the Lord him - self com - pare?
3 O thou Je - ho-vah, God of hosts, What migh-ty one thy like - ness boasts?

Thy faith-ful-ness shall praise com-mand, When ho - ly ones as - sem - bled stand.
Or who, a-mong the migh - ty, shares The like-ness that Je - ho - vah bears?
Thy faith-ful-ness is ev - er found, En - cir-cling all thy path a - round.

Ps.90th, 6-8. L. M. 6 lines.

By per. THEO. E. PERKINS.

1 O teach thou us to count our days, And set our hearts on wis-dom's ways.
2 O do thy mer-cy soon im-part To sat-is-fy our long-ing heart,
3 Thy work un-to thy ser-vants show, Thy glo-ry let their chil-dren know,

Re-turn, O Lord, at length re-lent, And for thy ser-vants' sake re-pent.
So we re-joice shall all our days, And hap-py be in thee al-ways.
And let there be on us bestowed The beau-ty of the Lord our God:

How long—how long—thus shall it be? Re-turn, that we may joy in thee.
For days of grief that we have had, And years of e-vil make us glad.
The work ac-com-plished by our hand Let it by thee es-tab-lished stand.

How long—how long—thus shall it be? Re-turn, that we may joy in thee.
For days of grief that we have had, And years of e-vil make us glad.
The work ac-com-plished by our hand Let it by thee es-tab-lished stand.

No. 96. PERFECT SECURITY.

Ps. 91st, 1-4. L. M.

FRANK M. DAVIS.

1 The man who once has found a-bode With-in the se-cret place of God,
2 I of the Lord my God will say, He is my ref-uge and my stay;
3 He shall with all pro-tect-ing care Pre-serve thee from the fowl-er's snare;
4 His outspread pin-ions shall thee hide; Be-neath his wings shalt thou con-fide;

Shall with al-migh-ty God a-bide, And in his sha-dow safe-ly hide.
To him for safe-ty I will flee; My God, in him my trust shall be.
When fearful plagues a-round pre-vail, No fa-tal stroke shall thee as-sail.
His faith-ful-ness shall ev-er be A shield and buck-ler un-to thee.

No. 97. RINDGE.

Ps. 92d, 11, 12. C. M.

1 But like the palm-tree flour-ish-ing Shall be the right-eous one;
2 Those that with-in the house of God Are plant-ed by his grace,

And he shall like the ce-dar grow That is in Leb-a-non.
They shall grow up, and flour-ish all In our God's ho-ly place.

And he shall like the ce-dar grow That is in Leb-a-non.
They shall grow up, and flour-ish all In our God's ho-ly place.

No. 98. DELLFONT.

Ps. 93d, 1-5. C. M.

Spirited.

1 Je-ho-vah reigns, and clothed is he With ma-jes-ty most bright;
  Him-self Je-ho-vah clothes with strength And girds a-bout with might.
2 The floods, O Lord, have lift-ed up, They lift-ed up their voice;
  The floods have lift-ed up their waves, And made a migh-ty noise.

The world is al-so firm-ly fixed, That it can-not de-part.
But yet the Lord, that is on high, Is migh-ti-er by far
Thy tes-ti-mo-nies ev'-ry one In faith-ful-ness ex-cel;

Thy throne is fixed of old, and thou From ev-er-last-ing art.
Than noise of ma-ny wa-ters is, Or great sea-bil-lows are.
And ho-li-ness for-ev-er, Lord, Thy house be-com-eth well.

No. 99. O COME, LET US SING.

Ps. 95th, 1, 2. L. M. 6 lines.

By per. W. T. WILEY.

1 O come, and let us sing to God, The rock of our sal-va-tion laud;
2 The vast deep pla-ces of the land, And strength of hills are in his hand;

Let us in psalms our tongues employ; Be-fore him render thanks with joy;
The sea is his, he gave it birth, His hands prepared the sol-id earth:

The Lord is great whose praise we sing,
O come, and let us wor-ship now,

The Lord is great whose praise we sing, The Lord is great whose praise we sing,
O come, and let us wor-ship now, O come, and let us wor-ship now,

The Lord is great whose praise we sing, A-bove all gods a migh-ty King.
O come, and let us worship now, Be-fore the Lord our Maker bow.

Ps. 96th, 1-4. L. M.

No. 100. MASON.

S. F.

1 O sing a new song to the Lord; Sing all the earth and bless his name.
2 Tell all the world his won-drous ways, Tell heathen na-tions far and near;
3 The heathen gods are i-dols vain; He made the heavens, and he sup-ports.
4 O give the Lord, ye tribes and tongues, O give the Lord due praise and sing.

From day to day his praise re-cord, The Lord's re-deem-ing grace pro-claim.
Great is the Lord, and great his praise, Feared more than gods that na-tions fear.
Both light and hon-or lead his train, While strength and beau-ty fill his courts.
Give strength and glory in your songs, Come, throng his courts, and off'-rings bring.

No. 101. LET EARTH BE GLAD.

Ps. 98th, 1, 2, 4, 6. L. M.

S. T. Wallace.

1 Come, let us sing unto the Lord, New songs of praise with sweet ac - cord;
2 The great sal-va - tion of our God Is seen thro' all the earth a - broad;
3 All lands, to God lift up your voice; Sing praise to him, with shouts re - joice;

For won-ders great by him are done; His hand and arm have vic-t'ry won.
Be-fore the heath-en's wondering sight, He hath revealed his truth and right.
With voice of joy and loud ac - claim, Let all u - nite and praise his name.

CHORUS.

Let earth be glad, ... let bil - lows roar, ... And all that

Let earth be glad, let bil - low's roar,

dwell . . . . from shore to shore; . . . . Let floods clap

And all that dwell from shore to shore;

hands . . . with one ac - cord, Let hills re-joice, be fore the Lord.

Let floods clap hands with one ac-cord, Let hills re-joice, rejoice be-fore the Lord.

No. 102. RELIGION AT HOME.

Ps. 101st, 1-4. 7s & 6s.

By per. Geo. B. Loomis.

1 Of mer - cy and of judg - ment, O Lord, I'll sing to thee. In wisdom and up-
2 No work of sin I'll suf - fer Be - fore my eyes to be; I hate the work of

right - ness Shall my be - ha-viour be. O when wilt thou, Je-ho - vah, To
sin - ners, It shall not cleave to me, The man whose heart is fro - ward, Shall

me in kind-ness come ? With heart sin-cere and per - fect I'll walk with-in my home.
from my pres - ence go. None who in sin takes pleas - ure Will I con-sent to know.

No. 103. SING A NEW SONG.

Ps. 98th, 1-4. 8s & 7s.

H. B. ALLEN.

1 Lo, Je-ho - vah his sal - va-tion Hath to all the world made known;
2 Mind-ful of his truth and mer - cy He to Isr' - el's house hath been,
3 All the earth, sing to Je-ho - vah, Shout a - loud, sing and re - joice;

In the sight of ev' - ry na - tion He his right-eous-ness hath shown.
And the Lord our God's sal - va - tion All the ends of earth have seen.
With the harp sing to Je-ho - vah, With the harp and tune - ful voice.

CHORUS.

Sing a new song to Je-ho - vah, For the won - ders he hath wrought;

His right hand and arm, most ho - ly, Vic - to - ry to him have brought.

No 104. JEHOVAH REIGNS.

Ps. 99th, 1-4. C. M.

J. C. MACY.

1 The Lord Je - ho - vah reigns as King, Let all the peo - ple quake:
2 The King's strength judgment al - so loves; Thou set - tlest e - qui - ty:

He sits be-tween the cher - u - bim, Let earth be moved and shake.
Thou judg - ment just dost ex - e - cute In Ja - cob right - eous - ly.

Je - ho - vah is in Zi - on great, A - bove all peo - ple high;
The Lord our God ex - alt on high, And rev' - rent - ly do ye

Thy fear - ful. great, and ho - ly name, O let them mag - ni - fy.
Be - fore his foot - stool wor - ship him: The Ho - ly One is he.

No. 105. PRAISE.

Ps. 100th, 1-4. 8s.

C. E. POLLOCK.

Animated.

1 All peo - ple that dwell on the earth, Your songs to Je - ho - vah now raise;
2 O en - ter his tem - ple with praise, His por - tals with thank-ful ac-claim;

O wor-ship Je - ho - vah with mirth, Approach him with anthems of praise.
Your voic - es in thanksgiv - ing raise; And bless ye his glo - ri - ous name.

Know ye that Je - ho - vah is God, Our Sov'-reign and Ma-ker is he;
For good is Je - ho - vah the Lord, His mer - cy to us nev - er ends;

His peo-ple who bow to his rod, And sheep of his pas ture are we.
His faith-ful-ness true to his word, Thro' a - ges un -end - ing ex - tends.

No. 106. MESSIAH.

Ps. 102d, 9-12. 7s.

HAROLD.

1 Thou shalt now for Zi - on rise, View - ing her with pity - ing eyes;
2 Zi - on's walls built up shall be; All shall then God's glo - ry see.

Now shall Zi - on fa - vor see, 'Tis the time de - creed by thee.
He the des - ti - tute shall hear, And will not de - spise their prayer.

For thy saints thy prom - ise trust, Lov - ing ev'n her stones and dust.
Of this truth shall re - cord be, That the com - ing race may see.

So shall hea - then fear God's name; All earth's kings thy glo - rious fame.
God shall in - to be - ing bring, Peo - ple, that his praise shall sing.

No. 107. WHAT A FRIEND WE HAVE IN JESUS.

Ps. 103d, 1-6. 8s & 7s.   By per. CHAS. C. CONVERSE.

1 O my soul, bless thou Je-ho - vah, All with - in me bless his name;
2 Who with ten-der mer-cies crowns thee, Who with good things fills thy mouth,
3 He made known his ways to Mo - ses, And his acts to Is - r'el's race;

Bless Je-ho - vah, and for - get not All his mer-cies to pro-claim.
So that ev - en like the ea - gle Thou hast been restored to youth.
God is plen-ti-ful in mer - cy, Slow to an-ger, rich in grace.

Who forgives all thy transgress - ions, Thy dis-eas-es all who heals;
In his righteousness, Je-ho - vah Will de-liv-er those distressed.
He will not for-ev-er chide us, Nor keep an-ger in his mind,

Who redeems thee from destruc - tion, Who with thee so kind-ly deals.
He will ex-e-cute just judg - ment In the cause of all oppressed.
Hath not dealt as we of-fend - ed, Nor re-ward-ed as we sinned.

No. 108. GOD UNCHANGEABLE.

Ps. 102d, 17-20. 7s.   From "CRYSTAL SONGS," by per.   S. WESLEY MARTIN.

1 Lord, thy years with - out an end Through the a - ges all ex - tend.
2 They shall speed - i - ly de-cay, But thy years shall last for aye;
3 As a ves - ture shall they be, They shall all be changed by thee;
4 Chil - dren of thy her - i - tage Shall en - dure through ev' - ry age,

Earth's foun-da - tions thou hast laid; Thou of old the heavens hast made.
Yea, the works we now be-hold All like gar-ments shall wax old.
Yet unchanged, as years ex - tend, Thy years, Lord, shall have no end.
And their sons from race to race Shall not fail be - fore thy face.

No. 109. BLESSED BE JEHOVAH.

Ps. 106th, 38. C. M.   By per. Rev. D. A. Duff.

Blessed be Jeho-vah, Is - r'el's God, To all e - ter - ni - ty, Let

all the peo - ple say, A - men. Let all the peo - ple say, A - men. Let

A - men.   A - men.

cres.

all the peo - ple say, A - men. Praise to the Lord give ye.

No. 110. ANTIOCH.

Ps. 104th, 26, 28, 29. C. M.   Handel, arr. by Dr. L. Mason.

1 The glo - ry of the migh - ty Lord For - ev - er shall en - dure; And in his
2 I to the Lord Most High will sing So long as I shall live; And while I
3 Of him my me - di - ta - tion shall Sweet thoughts to me af - ford; And as for

works Je - ho - vah shall   Re - joice for - ev - er - more,   Re -
be - ing have I will   To my God prais - es give,   To
me, I will re - joice   In God, my on - ly Lord,   In

joice for - ev - er - more,   Re - joice, Re - joice for - ev - er - more.
my God prais - es give,   To my God, To my God prais - es give.
God, my on - ly Lord,   In God, In God, my on - ly Lord.

No. 111. GIVE THANKS.

Ps. 106th, 1-4. C. M.

E. O. Butterfield.

1 God's migh-ty works who can ex-press? Or show forth all his praise?
2 Re-mem-ber me, O Lord, with love, Which thou to thine dost bear;
3 That I thy cho-sen's good may see, And in their joy re-joice;

O blest are they that judg-ment keep, And just-ly do al-ways.
With thy sal-va-tion, O my God, To vis-it me draw near.
And may with thine in-her-it-ance Ex-ult with cheer-ful voice.

CHORUS.

Praise ye . . . the Lord, . .

Praise ye the Lord, and give him thanks, For boun-ti-ful is he;

His mer-cy shall en-dure, . .

His ten-der mer-cy shall en-dure To all e-ter-ni-ty.

No. 112. HOW BLEST.

Ps. 112th, 1-3, 6. L. M.

German. Arr. by W. H. Monks.

1 How blest the man that fears the Lord, And makes his law his chief de-light;
2 A-bound-ing wealth shall bless his home, His right-eous ness shall still en-dure,
3 The good will fa-vor show, and lend, And his af-fairs dis-creet-ly guide;
4 The wick-ed shall his hon-or see, Con-sume with grief, and gnash and wail;

His seed shall share his great re-ward, And on the earth be men of might.
To him shall light a-rise in gloom; He's kind, com-pas-sion-ate and pure.
Un-moved he stands till life shall end, His name and hon-or shall a-bide.
Their hopes shall dis-ap-point-ed be, And their de-sires for-ev-er fail.

No. 113. O PRAISE THE LORD.

Ps. 107th, 1-5. C. M.

By per. Frank M. Davis.

1 O Praise the Lord, for he is good; His mer - cies last - ing be.
2 He gather - ed them from all the lands, From north, south, east, and west.
3 Their wea - ry soul with - in them faints, When thirst and hun - ger press;
4 Them al - so in a way to walk That right is he doth guide,

Let God's re - deem - ed say so, whom he From pow'r of foes set free.
They strayed in de - sert's path - less way, No ci - ty found to rest.
In trou - ble then they cry to God, He frees them from dis - tress.
That they may to a ci - ty go, Where - in they may a - bide.

CHORUS.

O that men to the Lord would give Praise for his good - ness then, Praise for his

O that men to the Lord would give, O that men to the Lord would give,

good - ness then, And for his works of won - der done Un - to the sons of men!

wonder done.

Ps. 116, 1-3, 5. C. M. ## No. 114. CROSS AND CROWN.

1 I love the Lord, be - cause my voice And pray - ers he did hear.
2 Of death the cords and sor - rows did A - bout me com - pass round;
3 Up - on the name of God the Lord I then did call, and say,
4 O thou my soul, do thou re - turn Un - to thy qui - et rest;

I, while I live, will call on him, Who bowed to me his ear.
The pains of hell took hold on me, I grief and trou - ble found.
De - liv - er thou my soul, O Lord, I do thee hum - bly pray.
For, large - ly, un - to thee, the Lord His boun - ty hath ex - pressed.

66

No. 115. MY HEART IS FIXED.

Ps. 108th, 1-4. C. M.

E. B. SMITH.

1 My heart is fixed, O Lord; I'll sing, And with my glo-ry praise. A-wake both psal-ter-
2 Be thou a-bove the heavens, Lord, Ex-alt-ed ve-ry high, And far a-bove the

y and harp; My-self I'll ear-ly raise. I'll praise thee 'mong the people, Lord; 'Mong
earth do thou Thy glo-ry mag-ni-fy; That thy be-lov-ed peo-ple may From

na-tions sing will I: Above the heav'ns thy mercy's great, Thy truth doth reach the sky.
bondage be set free: O do thou save with thy right hand, And answer give to me.

No. 116. JEFFERSON STREET.

Ps. 110th, 1-3. L. P. M.

1 Je-ho-vah to my Lord thus spake, Till I thy foes thy foot-stool make,
2 Thee, in thy power's tri-umph-ant day, The will-ing na-tions shall o-bey;
3 The Lord un-chang-ing oath has made, "Mel-chi-se-dec's thy priest-ly grade,

Sit thou in state at my right hand; God shall from Zi-on send a-broad
And when thy ris-ing beams they view, Shall all redeemed from er-ror's night,
In ev-er-last-ing priest-hood crowned;" The sovereign Lord at thy right hand,

O'er na-tions all thy migh-ty rod, A-mid thy foes thy throne shall stand.
Ap-pear as num-ber-less and bright As crys-tal drops of morn-ing dew.
Shall strike thro' prin-ces of the land, While aw-ful an-ger flames a-round.

No. 117. THE LORD PROVIDES.

Ps. 111th, 5-8. C. M.   C. E. POLLOCK.

1 { The Lord pro-vi-deth food for all, Who do him tru-ly fear; }
{ And ev-er-more his cov-e-nant He in his mind will bear. }
2 { His hands' works all are truth and right; All his com-mands are sure: }
{ And, done in truth and up-right-ness, They ev-er-more en-dure. }

He did the pow-er of his works To his own peo-ple show, That
He to his cho-sen peo-ple sent Re-demp-tion by his pow'r; His

he the hea-then's her-i-tage Up-on them might be-stow.
cov-e-nant he did com-mand To be for-ev-er-more.

No. 118. ANDRE.

Ps. 113th, 1-3. L. M.   By per. W. B. BRADBURY.

1 Praise God, ye ser-vants of the Lord, Praise, praise his name with
2 From ris-ing un-to set-ting sun, Praised be the Lord, the
3 O who is like the Lord, our God, Who makes the heav-ens

one ac-cord; Bless ye the Lord, his name a-dore From this time
migh-ty one. O'er na-tions all God reigns su-preme, A-bove the
his a-bode; Who stoops to see from his high throne What things in

forth for-ev-er-more, From this time forth for-ev-er-more.
heavens his glo-ries beam, A-bove the heavens his glo-ries beam.
heaven and earth are done? What things in heaven and earth are done?

No. 119. GOD'S BLESSINGS.

Ps. 115th, 7-10. C. M.

D. C. JOHN.

1 The Lord of us hath mind-ful been, And he will bless us still;
2 Yea tru - ly blest are ye of God, Who made the earth and heav'n.

He will the house of Is - r'el bless, Bless Aa - ron's house he will.
The heav'n, ev'n heav'ns, are God's but he Earth to men's sons hath giv'n.

Both small and great, that fear the Lord, He will them sure - ly bless.
The dead, and who to si - lence go, God's praise do not re - cord.

The Lord will you, you and your seed, Still more and more in - crease.
But hence - forth we for - ev - er will Bless God. Praise ye the Lord.

CHORUS.

Praise ye the Lord, ... Praise ye the Lord, ... Praise
Praise ye the Lord, Praise ye the Lord,

ye, praise ye the Lord. But henceforth we for - ev - er will bless God. Praise ye the Lord.

No. 120. HAMBURG.

Ps. 116th, 7-11. L. M.

Arr. by Dr. L. Mason.

1 What fit re - turn, Lord, can I make For all thy gifts on me be - stowed?
2 Be - fore God's peo - ple I'll ap - pear, And pay my vows there with de - light.
3 O Lord, the high and ho - ly one, I am a ser - vant un - to thee,
4 With sac - ri - fice of thanks I'll go, And on Je - ho - vah's name will call;
5 Yea, I will pay my vows to God, In midst of thee, Je - ru - sa - lem.

The cup - of bless - ing I will take, And call up - on the name of God.
The death of saints to God is dear, Most pre - cious in Je - ho - vah's sight.
Thy ser - vant and thy hand-maid's son, Thou hast from bonds de - liv - ered me.
Will pay to God the vows I owe, In pres - ence of his peo - ple all.
With - in the courts of God's a - bode, Praise ye Je - ho - vah, praise his name.

No. 121. HALLELUJAH.

Ps. 117th, 1, 2. 8s & 7s.

P. P. Bliss.

1 Praise Je - ho - vah, all ye na - tions, All ye peo - ple, praise pro - claim;
2 Great to us hath been his mer - cy, Ev - er faith - ful is his word;

For his grace and lov ing-kind - ness, O sing prais - es to his name.
Through all a - ges it en - dur - eth, Hal - le - lu - jah, praise the Lord.

CHORUS.

Hal - le - lu - jah, hal - le - lu - jah, Hal - le - lu - jah, praise the Lord;

Great to us hath been his mer - cy, Ev - er faith - ful is his word.

No. 122. BETTER TO TRUST.

Ps. 118th, 1-5. L. M.

By per. E. MANFORD CLARK.

1 The Lord is good; O bless his name; His mer-cy ev-er is the same,
2 Let Aa-ron's house this truth de-clare; Je-ho-vah's mer-cies end-less are.
3 I called on God in time of grief; He heard my prayer, and sent re-lief.
4 The Lord doth take my part with those Who give me help a-gainst my foes;

And let the house of Is-r'el say, His ten-der mer-cy lasts for aye.
Let all that fear the Lord pro-claim, His mer-cy ev-er is the same.
The Lord to res-cue me is near; What man can do I will not fear.
I my de-sire shall therefore see On those who ha-tred bear to me.

CHORUS.

Bet-ter to trust the Lord Most High, Than on the help of man re-ly.

Bet-ter to trust Je-ho-vah's grace, Than con-fi-dence in prin-ces place.

Ps. 119th, 7-9, 12. C. M.

No. 123. HERBERT.

1 By what means shall a young man learn His way to cleanse, O Lord?
2 Un-feign-ed-ly thee have I sought With all my soul and heart:
3 Thy word I in my heart have hid That I of-fend not thee.
4 Up-on thy stat-utes my de-light Shall con-stant-ly be set.

By tak-ing care-ful heed to it, Ac-cord-ing to thy word, Ac-cord-ing to thy word.
O nev-er let me from the path Of thy commands de-part, Of thy commands de-part.
O Lord, thou ev-er bles-sed art Thy sta-tutes teach thou me, Thy statutes teach thou me.
And by thy grace I nev-er will Thy ho-ly law for-get, Thy ho-ly law for-get.

No. 124. BELIEVE.

Ps. 119th, 73, 77, 78. C. M.

1 O how I love thy law! it is My stu-dy all the day:
2 How sweet un-to my taste, O Lord, Are all thy words of truth!
3 I through thy pre-cepts that are pure, Do un-der-stand-ing get;

It makes me wi-ser than my foes; For it doth with me stay.
Yea, I do find them sweet-er far Than hon-ey to my mouth.
I therefore ev'-ry way that's false With all my heart do hate.

No. 125. CANAAN.

Ps. 119th, 97-100. C. M.

1 Thy sta-tutes, Lord, are won-der-ful; My soul them keeps with
2 Lord, look on me, and mer-ci-ful Do thou un-to me

care. The entrance of thy word gives light, Makes wise who sim-ple are.
prove, As thou art wont to do to those Thy name who tru-ly love.

My mouth I al-so open-ed wide, And pant-ed ear-nest-
O let my foot-steps in thy word A-right still or-dered

ly, While af-ter thy com-mand-ments all, I longed ex-ceed-ing-ly.
be: Let no in-i-qui-ty ob-tain Do-min-ion o-ver me.

No. 126. THORNTON.

By per. T. E. PERKINS.

Ps. 119th, 127, 130-132. C. M.

1 { O let my ear-nest pray'r and cry Come near be-fore thee, Lord;
Give un-der-stand-ing un-to me, Ac-cord-ing to thy word. }
2 { My soul re-vive, and then it shall Give prais-es un-to thee;
And let thy judg-ments ev-er-more Be help-ful un-to me. }

O let thy hand bring help to me: Thy pre-cepts are my choice.
I, like a lost sheep, went a-stray; Thy ser-vant seek and find:

I longed for thy sal-va-tion, Lord, And in thy law re-joice.
For thy com-mand-ments all, O Lord, I ev-er keep in mind.

No. 127. THE PERFECT WAY.

J. H. TENNEY.

Ps. 119th, 25-28. C. M.

1 Teach me, O Lord, the per-fect way Of thy com-mands di-vine; And to ob-serve it
2 In thy law's path make me to go: For I de-light there-in. My heart un-to thy

to the end I will my heart in-cline. Give un-der-stand-ing un-to me, So
pre-cepts turn, And not to world-ly gain. O do thou turn a-way mine eyes From

keep thy law shall I; I'll with in-teg-ri-ty of heart Ob-serve it care-ful-ly.
view-ing van-i-ty; And in thy good and ho-ly way Be pleased to quick-en me.

No. 128. HE SLUMBERS NOT.

Ps. 121st, 1-4. C. M.

1 { I to the hills will lift mine eyes, From whence doth come mine aid.
My safe-ty com-eth from the Lord, Who heav'n and earth hath made. }

2 { The Lord thee keeps, the Lord thy shade On thy right hand doth stay:
The moon by night thee shall not smite, Nor yet the sun by day. }

Thy foot he'll not let slide, nor will He slum-ber that thee keeps.
The Lord shall keep thy soul; he shall Pre-serve thee from all ill.

Be-hold, he that keeps Is-ra-el, He slum-bers not, nor sleeps.
Hence forth thy go-ing out and in God keep for-ev-er will.

No. 129. GOD SHIELDS THE RIGHTEOUS.

Ps. 125th, 1, 2, 4, 5. 7s & 6s.

1 He that in God con-fid-eth, Like Zi-on Mount shall be. Which ev-er-more a-
2 Thy good-ness, Lord, our Sa-viour, To all the good im-part; And ev-er show thy

bid-eth Un-moved e-ter-nal-ly. As moun tains, which de-fend her, Je-
fa-vor To men of up-right heart. But those whose choice is rath-er In

ru-sa-lem sur-round, His saints se-cure to rend-er God com-pas-seth a-round.
crooked ways to go; With sin-ners God shall gath-er On Israel peace be-stow.

No. 130. TO THE HILLS.

Ps. 121st, 1-4. 7s.

By per. P. J. SPRAGUE.

1 To the hills I'll lift mine eyes, Whence my hopes of suc-cor rise:
2 God thy keep-er still shall stand, As a shade on thy right hand;

From the Lord comes all my aid, Who the earth and heav'n hath made.
Nei-ther sun by day shall smite, Nor the si-lent moon by night.

He will ev-er be thy guide, And thy foot shall nev-er slide;
God shall guard from ev'-ry ill, Keep thy soul in safe-ty still;

God his Is-ra-el that keeps, Nev-er slum-bers, nev-er sleeps,
Both with-out and in thy door, He will keep thee ev-er-more.

No. 131. MIGDOL.

Ps. 122d, 1-5. L. M.

DR. L. MASON.

1 With joy I hear my friends ex-claim, "Come let us in God's tem-ple meet."
2 A ci-ty built com-pact and fair, Je-rus'-lem stands, the sa-cred place
3 'Tis there by his com-mand they meet, To ren-der thanks and pay their vows;
4 Pray that Je-rus' lem's peace en-dure, For all that love thee God will bless;
5 For sake of friends and kin-dred dear, My heart's de-sire is "peace to thee;"

Within thy gates, Je-ru-sa-lem, Shall ev-er stand our wil-ling feet.
To which the gath'ring tribes repair, Tribes of Je-ho-vah's cho-sen race.
And there is judgment's royal seat, There are the thrones of Da-vid's house.
Peace dwell within thy walls secure, And joy with-in thy pa-la-ces.
And for the house of God, my prayer Shall seek thy good con-tin-ual-ly.

No. 132. BLEST THE MAN WHO FEARS JEHOVAH. 75

Ps. 128th, 1-4. 8s & 7s.　　　　　　　　　　By per. J. Wm. Slaugenhaup.

1 Blest the man who fears Je - ho - vah, Walk - ing ev - er in his ways;
2 Lo, on him that fears Je - ho - vah, Shall this bles sed - ness at tend;

Thou shalt eat of thy hands' la - bor And be hap - py all thy days.
Thus Je - ho - vah out of Zi - on Shall to thee his bless - ings send.

Like a vine in fruit a - bound - ing, In thy house thy wife is found,
Thou shalt see Je - rus'-lem pros - per, Long as thou on earth shalt dwell;

And like ol - ive-plants, thy chil - dren, Com - pass - ing thy ta - ble round.
Thou shalt see thy chil-dren's chil - dren, And the peace of Is-ra - el.

No. 133. TABLER.

Ps. 124th, 5. C. M.　　　　　　　　　By per. E. H. Frost.

1 Our sure and all - suf - fi - cient help Is in JE - HO -VAH'S name;

His name who did the heav'n cre - ate, And who the earth did frame.

No. 134. FROM THE DEPTHS.

Ps. 130th, 1-5. 8s & 7s.

By per. W. O. PERKINS.

1 From the depths do I in-voke thee, O Je-ho-vah, give an ear;
2 Lord, if thou shouldst mark trans-gres sions, Who, be-fore thee, Lord, shall stand?
3 For Je-ho-vah I am wait-ing, And my hope is in his word;
4 For the Lord my soul is wait-ing, More than watch-ers in the night,

To my voice be thou at-ten-tive, And my sup-pli-ca-tion hear.
But with thee there is for-give-ness, That thy name may fear com-mand.
In his word of promise giv-en, Yea, my soul waits for the Lord.
More than they for morning watch-ing, Watch-ing for the morn-ing light.

CHORUS.

Is-rael hope thou in Je-ho-vah, Mercies great are found with him;

He a-bound-ing in re-demp-tion, Is-r'el will from sin re-deem.

No. 135. SEYMOUR.

Ps. 126th, 1-3. L. M.

W. B. BRADBURY.

1 'Twas like a dream, when by the Lord From bond-age Zi-on
2 The heathen owned what God had wrought; Great works, which joy to
3 Who sow in tears, with joy shall reap; Though bear-ing pre-cious

ritard.

was restored: Our mouths were filled with mirth, our tongues Were ever singing joy-ful songs.
us have brought. As southern streams, when filled with rain, Lord, turn our captive state a gain.
seed they weep While going forth, yet shall they sing, When coming back their sheaves they bring.

No. 136. O THANK THE LORD OF LOVE.

Ps. 136th, 1-5. L. M.   E. L. M.

1 O   thank the Lord, the Lord of love; O   thank the God, all   gods a - bove.
2 O   thank the might - y King of kings, Whose arm hath done such won - drous things.
3 Whose wis dom gave the heavens their birth And   on   the wa - ters spread the earth.
4 Who taught yon glori - ous lights their way, The   ra - diant sun to   rule   the day.
5 The moon and stars   to   rule the night, With ra - diance of a   mild - er light.

His   mer - cy   flows   an end - less stream To   all   e - ter - ni - ty   the same.
His   mer - cy   flows   an end - less stream To   all   e - ter - ni - ty   the same.
His   mer - cy   flows   an end - less stream To   all   e - ter - ni - ty   the same.
His   mer - cy   flows   an end - less stream To   all   e - ter - ni - ty   the same.
His   mer - cy   flows   an end - less stream To   all   e - ter - ni - ty   the same.

CHORUS.

Thank   the Lord, the Lord   of Love; O   thank the God, all gods a - bove. His

Mer - cy   flows   an end - less stream, To   all   e - ter - ni - ty   the same.

Ps. 127th, 1-4. L. M.   ## No. 137. RETREAT.   T. Hastings.

Gentle.

1 Un - less   the Lord the house shall build,   The wea - ry build - ers   toil in vain.
2 In   vain you rise ere morn - ing break,   And late your night - ly   vi - gils keep,
3 Lo, chil - dren are   the gift   of God,   And sons the bless - ing   he com mands;
4 And hap - py they whose quiv - ers bear   Full store of ar - rows such as these;

Un - less the Lord the   ci - ty shield,   The guards a   use - less watch main-tain.
And bread of anx - ious care par-take: God gives to   his   be - lov - ed sleep.
These, when in youth - ful days be-stowed,   Are like the   shafts in   war - rior's hands,
They in   the   gate are free from fear,   And bold - ly   face their en - e - mies.

No. 138. FIRM AND SURE, ETERNALLY.

Ps. 136th, 1, 2, 4. H. M.

T. MARTIN TOWNE.

1 Praise God for he is kind: . . His mer-cy lasts for aye: . .
2 The Lord of lords praise ye . . . Whose mer-cies al - ways last: . .
3 To him great lights that made, . . The sun to rule by day; . .

is kind
praise ye
that made

Give thanks with heart and mind . . To God of gods al - way: . .
The Lord a - lone is he . . . Who do - eth won - ders vast.
The moon and stars ar - rayed; . . To rule the night are they. . .

and mind
is he
ar-rayed

CHORUS.

For cer-tain-ly His mer-cies dure Most firm and sure E - ter-nal-ly.

For cer-tain-ly His mer-cies dure Most firm and sure E - ter-nal-ly.

Ps. 132, 7, 8, 11. 8s & 7s.

No. 139. SICILIAN HYMN.

1 God hath sworn in truth to Da - vid, And his oath will not dis - own:
2 If thy sons will keep my cov' - nant And ob - serve what I com - mand,
3 There shall Da - vid's pow - er flour - ish, For my king a lamp's or - dained;

Of the chil - dren which I give thee, I will place up - on thy throne.
On thy throne for - ev - er sit - ting, Shall their chil - dren rule the land.
I with shame his foes will cov - er, But his crown shall be main - tained.

No. 140. MY REFUGE.

Ps. 142d, 1-4. L. M.

C. E. Pollock.

1 To God my earn-est voice I raise: To God my voice im-plor-ing prays:
2 When griefs my faint-ing soul o'er-flow, Thou know-est, Lord, the way I go.
3 All un-pro-tect-ed, lo, I stand; No friend-ly guard-ian at my hand;

Be-fore his face I pour my tears, And tell my sor-row in his ears.
And all the toils that foes do lay To snare thy ser-vant in his way.
No place of flight or ref-uge near, And none to whom my soul is dear.

CHORUS.

To Thee, To Thee, With-out a hope be-sides I flee;

O Lord, my Sa-viour, now to thee.

To Thee, To Thee, My por-tion in the land of life.

To thee my shel-ter from the strife.

No. 141. WOODWORTH.

Ps. 139th, 4-6, 8. L. M.

W. B. Bradbury. From "Psalmista."

1 O whith-er shall my foot-steps fly, Be-yond thy Spir-its search-ing eye?
2 If I to heav-en shall as-cend, Thy pres-ence there will me at-tend;
3 If on the morn-ing wings I flee, And dwell in ut-most parts of sea;
4 From thee the shades can nought dis-guise, The night is day be-fore thine eyes;

To what re-treat shall I re-pair, And find not thy dread pres-ence there?
If in the grave I make my bed, Lo, there I find thy pres-ence dread.
Even there thy hand shall guide my way, And thy right hand shall be my stay.
The dark ness is to thee as bright As are the beams of noon-day light.

No. 142. TEACH ME.

Ps. 143d. 9-11. C. M.

J. M. STILLMAN.

2 Teach me the way where I should go, I lift my soul to thee;
3 Be - cause thou art my God, I pray, Teach me to do thy will;
4 Re - vive me, Lord, for thy great name, And for thy judg-ment's sake;

Re - deem me from the rag - ing foe; To thee, O Lord, I flee.
O lead me in the per - fect way, By thy good Spir - it still.
From all my woes, O Lord, re - claim, My soul from trou - ble take.

To thee, O Lord, I flee, To thee, O Lord I flee;
By thy good spir - it still, By thy good Spir - it still;
My soul from trou - ble take, My soul from trou - ble take;

Re - deem me from the rag - ing foe; To thee, O Lord, I flee.
O lead me in the per - fect way, By thy good Spir - it still.
From all my woes, O Lord, re - claim, My soul from trou - ble take.

No. 143. ORLAND.

Ps. 141st, 1-3. L. M.

Dr. Arnold.

1 O Lord, my God, to thee I cry; Swift to my aid in mer - cy fly;
2 As fra - grant in - cense on the air, So mount to heaven my ear - ly prayer;
3 Set, Lord, a watch my mouth be - fore, And of my lips keep thou the door.

And when to thee my cries as - cend, In pi - ty to my voice at - tend,
And let my hands up - lift - ed be, As eve - ning sac - ri - fice to thee.
Nor leave my sin - ful heart to stray Where e - vil foot - steps lead the way.

No. 144. GOD IS KING.

Ps. 146th, 1, 3-6. 8s & 7s.   By per. A. J. Abbey.

1 He that hath the God of Ja - cob   For his help is tru - ly blest;
2 On the Lord who made the heav-en   Earth and sea, and all there - in;
3 He gives food to those that hun ger,   To the blind re-stor-eth sight.
4 He the right-eous loves, and safe-ly,   Keeps the stranger; he's a stay

He whose hope is in Je - ho - vah,   And up-on his God doth rest;
Who will keep his truth for ev - er,   Rights of all oppressed main tain.
He gives freedom to the pris' - ner,   Makes the bowed to stand up - right.
To the fath-er-less and wi - dow,   But sub-verts the sin ners way.

CHORUS.

Hal-le-lu - jah! praise Je-ho-vah, O my soul, Je-ho-vah praise;

While I live I'll praise Je - ho - vah, To my God sing all my days.

No. 145. TO THEE I PRAY.

Ps. 143, 6, 7, 10, 12. 6s.   Wm. B. Bradbury.

1 To thee I stretch my hands;   Do thou my help - er be:
2 O Lord, send quick re - lief,   I hum - bly pray to thee.
3 Cause me to know the way   In which my path should be;
4 Thou art my God in need,   Teach me thy just com - mand,

As long the thirst - ing lands,   So longs my soul for thee.
My spir - it fails through grief,   Thy face hide not from me.
Be - cause to thee I pray,   And lift my soul to thee.
Thy Spir - its good; me lead   In - to the per - fect land.

No. 146. PRAISE, PRAISE.

Ps. 148th, 1-3, 5-8. 8s & 7s.

C. E. POLLOCK.

1 Hal - le - lu - jah, praise Je - ho - vah, From the heav-ens praise his name; Praise Je-
2 All ye fruit - ful trees and ce - dars, All ye hills and moun-tains high, Creep-ing
3 Let them prais - es give Je - ho - vah, For his name a - lone is high. And his

ho - vah in the high - est, All his an - gels praise pro-claim. All his
things, and beasts and cat - tle, Birds that in the heav - ens fly. Kings of
glo - ry is ex - alt - ed Far a - bove the earth and sky He his

hosts to - geth - er praise him, Sun, and moon, and stars on high; Praise him,
earth, and all ye peo - ple, Prin - ces great, earth's judg - es all; Praise his
peo - ple's pow'r ex - alt - eth, All his saints to praise ac - cord; Ja - cob's

O ye heav'ns of heav - ens All ye floods a - bove the sky
name, young men and maid - ens, A - ged men and chil - dren small,
seed, a peo - ple near him. Hal - le - lu - jah. Praise the Lord.

CHORUS.

Praise, praise, praise, Let them prais - es give Je - ho - vah; Praise, praise, praise, They were

made at his com - mand, Them for - ev - er he es - tab - lish'd, for ev - er he es - tab - lished; His de - cree shall ev - er stand.

Ps. 145th, 11-14. L. M.

No. 147. AMES.

DR. LOWELL MASON.

1 The Lord is just in his ways all, And ho - ly in his works each one.
2 God will the just de - sire ful - fil Of such as do him fear in - deed.
3 The Lord will keep con - tin - ual - ly All who him love with up - right heart;
4 My mouth and lips I'll there - fore frame, To speak the prais - es of the Lord:

The Lord is near to all who call, Who call in truth on him a - lone.
Their cry re - gard, and hear he will, And save them in the time of need.
But all who work in - i - qui - ty De-stroy will he, and quite sub - vert.
To mag - ni - fy his ho - ly name For - ev - er let all flesh ac - cord.

No. 148. PREPARE YOUR GLAD VOICE.

Ps. 149th, 1-4. 10s & 11s.

By per. J. H. FILLMORE.

1 O praise ye the Lord! Pre-pare your glad voice, New songs with his saints,
2 And let them his name Ex - tol in the dance, With tim - brel and harp
3 His saints shall sing loud With glo - ry and joy, And rest un - dis mayed,
4 The heath-en to judge, Their pride to con-sume; To fet - ter their kings,

As - sem - bled to sing; Be - fore his Cre - a - tor Let Is - rael re-
His prais - es ex - press; Who al - ways takes pleas - ures His saints to ad-
With songs in the night; The praise of Je - ho - vah Their lips shall em-
Their prin - ces to bind; To ex - e - cute on them The long - de - creed

joice, And chil - dren of Zi - on Be glad in their King.
vance, And with his sal - va - tion The hum - ble to bless.
ploy; A sword in their right hand, Two - edged for the fight.
doom; Such hon - or, for - ev - er The ho - ly shall find.

No. 149. PRAISE YE THE LORD.

Ps. 147th, 1, 3, 4. C. M.   C. F. POLLOCK.

1 Praise ye the Lord; for it is good Praise to our God to sing:
2 Those that are brok-en in their heart, And trou-bled in their minds,
3 He counts the num-ber of the stars; He names them ev'-ry one.

For it is pleas-ant, and to praise It is a come-ly thing.
He heal-eth, and their pain-ful wounds, He ten-der-ly up-binds.
Our Lord is great, and of great power, His wis-dom search can none.

CHORUS.

Praise the Lord, it is good Praise to our God to sing:

Praise ye the Lord, for it is good, Praise to sing,

For it is pleas-ant, and to praise It is a come-ly thing.

No. 150. PARTING HYMN.

Ps. 133d, 1, 3. C. M.   INGALLS.

1 { Behold how good a thing it is, And how be-com-ing well. }
  { To-geth-er such as breth-ren are In u-ni-ty to dwell. }   In u-ni-ty to
2 { As Hermon's dew, the dew that doth On Zi-on's hills de-scend: }
  { For there the blessing God commands Life that shall never end. } Life that shall never

dwell, In u-ni-ty to dwell. To-geth-er such as brethren are, In u-ni-ty to dwell.
end, Life that shall never end, For there the blessing God commands Life that shall never end.

ALPHABETICAL LIST OF SUBJECTS.

ALPHABETICAL LIST OF TUNES.

TUNE.	NO.	PS.	METRE.	VERSES.
Adullam	30	26	C. M.	2–5.
Agawam	24	23	C. M.	1–3, 5.
All glory to God	91	86	C. M.	6–11.
All lands to God	67	66	C. M.	1, 2, 3, 7.
Ames	147	145	L. M.	11–14.
Andre	118	113	L. M.	1–3.
Antioch	110	104	C. M.	26, 28, 29.
Apheka	65	57	C. M.	6, 8–10.
Ariel	68	63	C. P. M.	1–3.
Aylesbury	44	39	S. M.	8–11.
Bealoth	74	67	S. M.	1–4.
Believe	124	119	C. M.	73, 77, 78.
Better to trust Jehovah	122	118	L. M.	1–5.
Blessed be Jehovah	109	106	C. M.	38.
Blest the man who fears Jehovah	132	128	8s & 7s.	1–4.
Bow and Adore	34	29	12s & 11s.	1, 2, 5.
Bremen	11	12	C. P. M.	3, 4.
Brighton	10	10	S. M.	16–18.
Calm	20	17	C. H. M.	1–3.
Canaan	125	119	C. M.	97–100.
Clark	86	89	C. M.	15–18.
Converse	55	47	S. M.	1–5.
Coronation	79	72	C. M.	17, 18.
Cross and Crown	114	116	C. M.	1–3, 5.
Children, come	41	34	C. M.	7, 9, 11.
Dellfont	98	93	C. M.	1–5.
Deliver me	7	6	8s & 7s.	1, 2, 4, 5.
Downs	75	71	C. M.	1–4.
Enwood	6	4	L. M.	5–7.
Expostulation	26	24	11s.	1–3.
Fear the Lord	40	33	C. M.	7, 9–11.
Firm and sure, eternally	138	136	H. M.	1, 2, 4.
Freeport	35	31	S. M.	1–3, 5.
From the Depths	134	130	8s & 7s.	1–5.
Give ear	61	61	C. M.	1–4.
Give Thanks	111	106	C. M.	1–4.
God's Foundation	92	87	7s.	1, 2, 4, 5.
God is King	144	146	8s & 7s.	1, 3–6.
God our Refuge	51	46	C. M.	1–4.

TUNE.	NO.	PS.	METRE.	VERSES.
God shields the Righteous	129	125	7s & 6s.	1, 2, 4, 5.
God Unchangeable	108	102	7s.	17–20.
God will not Forsake	31	27	C. M.	9–12.
God's Blessings	119	115	C. M.	7–10.
Hallelujah	121	117	7s & 6s.	1, 2.
Hamburg	120	116	L. M.	7–11.
Hear, O Lord	3	5	7s.	1–3, 5, 6.
Hendon	2	2	7s.	5, 6, 8, 9.
Herbert	123	119	C. M.	7–9, 12.
He Slumbers Not	128	121	C. M.	1–4.
Hide not thy Face	77	69	S. M.	15–19.
Hinton	12	7	11s.	4–6.
How Blest	112	112	L. M.	1–3, 6.
How Long	13	13	7s & 6s.	1–6.
I cried to God	82	77	L. M.	1–3, 5.
I Hear Thy Welcome Voice	83	79	S. M.	8, 9, 11, 13.
In God we Boast	49	44	11s.	1, 2, 4.
In Thee I'm Trusting	43	38	8s & 7s.	10–13.
I love to tell the story	38	32	7s & 6s.	1, 2, 4–7.
Jefferson Street	116	110	L. P. M.	1–3.
Jehovah Reigns	104	99	C. M.	1–4.
Jesus' Cross	85	88	8s & 7s.	1–6.
Jesus of Nazareth passeth by	95	90	L. M.	6–8.
Keokuk	50	45	C. M.	13–17.
Laban	4	3	S. M.	2, 3, 5.
Let Earth be Glad	101	98	L. M.	1, 2, 4, 6.
Let Zion Rejoice	57	48	H. M.	1–3.
Lischer	19	19	H. M.	5–7.
Lord, Hear Me	17	17	C. M.	5–8.
Lord, Hasten to my Aid	47	40	C. M.	13 15, 18, 19
Lord God of Hosts, How Lovely	90	84	7s & 6s.	1–4, 9.
Lord our Lord	9	8	7s.	1–5.
Luther	62	53	S. M.	1–3, 7.
Lyra	42	36	C. M.	5–8.
Make Haste	80	70	11s & 8s.	1, 3, 4.
Market Square	28	25	S. M.	3–6.
Marsella	69	66	C. M.	12–14.
Mason	100	96	L. M.	1–4.
Meribah	37	31	C. P. M.	18, 19.
Messiah	106	102	7s.	9–12.
Migdol	131	122	L. M.	1–5.
My Heart is Fixed	115	108	C. M.	1–4.
My High Tower	14	18	L. M.	1, 2, 4.
My Refuge	140	142	L. M.	1–4.
O, Come let us Sing	99	95	L. M.	1, 2.
Olive's Brow	23	22	L. M.	15–17, 19.
O, Praise the Lord	113	107	C. M.	1–5.
Orland	143	141	L. M.	1–4.

TUNE.	NO.	PS.	METRE.	VERSES.
Ostend	88	84	C. M.	8–11.
O, Thou Shepherd of Israel	87	80	11s.	1, 2, 10.
O, Thank the Lord of Love	136	136	L. M.	1–5.
Parting Hymn	150	133	C. M.	1, 3.
Perfect Security	96	91	L. M.	1–4.
Portuguese Hymn	25	24	11s.	4–6.
Praise	105	100	8s.	1–4.
Praise, Praise	146	148	8s & 7s.	1–3, 5–8.
Praise Ye the Lord	149	147	C. M.	1, 3–4.
Praise Waits for Thee in Zion	70	65	7s & 6s.	1–6.
Prayer and Praise	32	28	S. M.	1–3, 6.
Prepare Your Glad Voice	148	149	10s & 11s.	1–4.
Ransom Me	29	25	7s.	12, 13, 15, 16
Religion at Home	102	101	7s & 6s.	1–4.
Remember Me	27	25	C. M.	1, 2, 5.
Rest	46	41	L. M.	1–3.
Rescue	18	18	C. M.	15–18.
Retreat	137	127	L. M.	1–4.
Rindge	97	92	C. M.	11, 12.
Rockingham	8	9	L. M.	5–8.
Rock of Ages	60	51	7s.	7–9.
Rothwell	84	76	L. M.	5–7.
Rowley	21	21	12s & 9s.	1–4.
Safely Guarded	5	5	7s.	9, 10.
Salem	76	68	7s & 6s.	32–35.
Salvation	63	54	S. M.	1–4.
Seymour	135	126	L. M.	1–3.
Sicillian Hymn	139	132	8s & 7s.	7, 8, 11.
Sing a New Song	103	98	8s & 7s.	1–4.
Silverton	64	56	C. M.	3, 8, 9.
Silver Street	58	50	S. M.	3–6.
St. Thomas	53	45	S. M.	3–7.
Tabler	133	124	C. M.	5.
Teach Me	142	143	C. M.	9–11.
The Ascended Saviour	73	68	7s & 6s.	17–20.
The Happy Man	1	1	C. M.	1–4.
The Lord is Great	56	48	S. M.	1, 2, 7–9.
The Lord Only	81	73	C. M.	19–23.
The Lord Provides	117	111	C. M.	5–8.
The Penitent	52	43	8s & 7s.	2–5.
The Perfect Way	127	119	C. M.	25–28.
The River Flows	54	46	8s & 6s.	2–4.
There is a Fountain	66	62	C. M.	1, 2, 7, 8.
Thornton	126	119	C. M.	127, 130–132.
To the Hills	130	121	7s.	1–4.
To Thee I Pray	145	143	6s.	6, 7, 9, 10, 12
Toy	48	42	8s & 4s.	1–4.
Trust His Love	16	16	S. M.	7–10.

TUNE.	NO.	PS.	METRE.	VERSES.
Trust in God	39	37	C. M.	3–6.
Turn us	89	85	L. P. M.	1–3.
Upton	94	89	L. M.	4, 5, 7.
Varina	72	68	C. M.	1, 3–5.
Waiting Patiently	45	40	C. M.	1–6.
Webb	71	65	7s & 6s.	9–12.
What a Friend we have in Jesus	107	103	8s & 7s.	1–6.
Whiter than Snow	59	51	7s.	1, 4, 5.
Who Shall Dwell?	15	15	7s.	1–5.
Why Me Forsake	93	88	8s & 7s.	7–12.
Why Stand Afar	22	22	L. M.	1–6.
With Songs I'll Thee Extol	36	30	7s & 6s.	1, 2, 5.
Woodworth	141	139	L. M.	4–6, 8.
Zebulon	33	27	H. M.	3–5.
Zerah	78	72	C. M.	6–9.

INDEX OF PSALMS.

PSALM.	METRE.	NO.	VERSES.	PSALM.	METRE.	NO.	VERSES.
1	C. M.	1	1-4.	34	C. M.	41	7, 9, 11.
2	7s.	2	5, 6, 8, 9.	36	C. M.	42	5-8.
3	S. M.	4	2, 3, 5.	37	C. M.	39	3-6.
4	L. M.	6	5, 6, 7.	38	8s & 7s.	43	10-13.
5	7s.	5	9, 10.	39	S. M.	44	8-11.
5	7s.	3	1-3, 5, 6.	40	C. M.	47	13-15, 18, 19.
6	8s & 7s.	7	1, 2, 4, 5.	40	C. M.	45	1-6.
7	11s.	12	4-6.	41	L. M.	46	1-3.
8	7s.	9	1-5.	42	8s & 4s.	48	1-4.
9	L. M.	8	5-8.	43	8s & 7s.	52	2-5.
10	S. M.	10	16-18.	44	11s.	49	1, 2, 4.
12	C. P. M.	11	3, 4.	45	C. M.	50	15-17.
13	7s & 6s.	13	1-6.	45	S. M.	53	3-7.
15	7s.	15	1-5.	46	8s & 6s.	54	2-4.
16	S. M.	16	7-10.	46	C. M.	51	1-4.
17	C. M.	17	5-8.	47	S. M.	55	1-5.
17	C. H. M.	20	1-3.	48	H. M.	57	1-3.
18	L. M.	14	1, 2, 4.	48	S. M.	56	1, 2, 7-9.
18	C. M.	18	15-18.	50	S. M.	58	3-6.
19	H. M.	19	5-7.	51	7s.	60	7-9.
21	12s & 9s.	21	1-4.	51	7s.	59	1, 4, 5.
22	L. M.	23	15-17, 19.	53	S. M.	62	1-3, 7.
22	L. M.	22	1-6.	54	S. M.	63	1-4.
23	C. M.	24	1-3, 5.	56	C. M.	64	3, 8, 9.
24	11s.	26	1-3.	57	C. M.	65	6, 8-10.
24	11s.	25	4-6.	61	C. M.	61	1-4.
25	S. M.	28	3-6.	62	C. M.	66	1, 2, 7, 8.
25	7s.	29	12, 13, 15, 16.	63	C. P. M.	68	1-3.
25	C. M.	27	1, 2, 5.	65	7s & 6s.	70	1-6.
26	C. M.	30	2-5.	65	7s & 6s.	71	9-12.
27	C. M.	31	9-12.	66	C. M.	69	12-14.
27	H. M.	33	3-5.	66	C. M.	67	1, 2, 3, 7.
28	S. M.	32	1-3, 6.	67	S. M.	74	1-4.
29	12s & 11s.	34	1, 2, 5.	68	C. M.	72	1, 3-5.
30	7s & 6s.	36	1-2, 5.	68	7s & 6s.	73	17-20.
31	S. M.	35	1-3, 5.	68	7s & 6s.	76	32-35.
31	C. P. M.	37	·18, 19.	69	S. M.	77	15-19.
32	7s & 6s.	38	1, 2, 4-7.	70	11s & 8s.	80	1, 3, 4.
33	C. M.	40	7, 9-11.	71	C. M.	75	1-4.

www.ingramcontent.com/pod-product-compliance
Lightning Source LLC
Chambersburg PA
CBHW020252290326
41930CB00039B/837